The Mystical Path of Christian Theosis

Practical Exercises For Experiencing Christian Purification, Illumination and Glorification

The Pathway to *Homo Deus*

Elijah John

MONASTIC PRESS

Monastic Press, An Imprint of
Top Shape Publishing
1135 Terminal Way #209
Reno, Nevada 85902

ISBN: 978-0-9998330-8-7
Library of Congress Number: 2020948361

DEDICATION

For all Christians, and especially the many Christian monastic traditions of monks and nuns who are fully devoted to the Gospel promise of spiritual union with God - *theosis* and *Homo Deus*. For those devoted to the pathway of Christian perfection, herein are the necessary spiritual exercises for passing through the stages of *catharsis (purgatio)*, *theoria* and *theosis* otherwise known as purification, illumination and glorification.

I particularly hope this information will be useful to African theologians who are starting to deeply study the pathway to *theosis* but struggling with charges that Christ is a western savior with a western identity rather than the universal example of God made man so that man might become a god. The necessary practice steps leading to divinization, deification, sanctification or *theosis* are herein covered for their benefit and the benefit of all Christians.

CONTENTS

ACKNOWLEDGMENTS

Christianity is much assaulted in today's world on a number of fronts. Many of its positive influences have been diminishing because people have lost faith in Christianity itself and its practices for salvation. Many have stopped believing in its promises of heavenly ascension and rejected the Church because they lack understanding of the pathway to *theosis* that is the second half of the sacrament of Baptism. This pathway is the actuality of Christianity.

Because the Christian monastic houses have enabled countless individuals to achieve *Homo Deus*, as testified by the holy lives and miraculous works of the saints, I am grateful for their present day existence and efforts to keep alive the pathway to *theosis*. I am also particularly grateful for the teachings that prior saints have left to us that can help guide us through *catharsis* and *theoria* to *theosis*. I hope this book will continue to aid the monastic houses in keeping open this pathway for all those who are pursuing the Christian spiritual pathway of salvation.

i

CHAPTER 1

CHRISTIANITY'S ULTIMATE PURPOSE IS *THEOSIS* AND *HOMO DEUS*

Sorrow, suffering and misfortune are everywhere in the world, but Heaven shines with resplendent glory and promise. Endlessly regenerating itself through continuous transformations, Heaven's grace is always within reach to help each of us also transform ourselves so that we might experience a higher, better existence. Should we not take advantage of Heaven's grace to transcend the world while within it and experience more of the divine? Christianity does so by offering us the divinization pathway of *theosis.*

Psalm 82:6 says, "Ye are gods." Basil of Alexandria said, "becoming a god is the highest goal of all." Saint Athanasius said, "He was incarnate that we might be made god." Clement of Alexandria said, "Yea, I say, the Word of God became a man so that you might learn from a man how to become a god." St. Thomas Aquinas wrote, "The only-begotten Son of God, wanting to make us sharers in his divinity, assumed our nature, so that he, made man, might make men gods." Saint Cyril said, "we shall become sons by participation."

What is it to "become a son by participation?" All Christians know that it is possible to join the community of saints by living a holy life of spiritual practice where we purify our bodies, minds and behaviors. We can through such efforts learn to transcend our lower nature - our passions and desires - to become what Jesus is Himself who partakes of the divine nature. This is, after all, the goal of the Christian life.

The goal of Christianity is that all of us become spiritualized, even divinized by spiritual efforts that will become blessed by help of the Holy Spirit. Nonetheless, that achievement of deification requires continual work we must personally do at a definite process of transformation. What is impure must become pure, what is evil must be rejected for the good, what is defiled must become incorrupt, what is lower must be discarded for the higher, what is dirty must become cleansed. As God's holiness is pure goodness, we must learn how to transcend what is base within us and elevate ourselves to a more perfect state, just as the glorified saints have done before us.

The unpurified man is not true to who he is, but acts outside of his true character. We must restore God's perfect image in ourselves and divinize our human nature to become our highest best self, our perfected self, our purified soul, our sacred self. We can do so by transcending the passion-ridden animal-like features of our personality, and then become a son by participation.

As Saint Irenaeus stated, "the Word became man, and the Son of God became the Son of man so that man, by entering into communion with the Word and thus receiving divine sonship, might become a son of God." This is becoming a son by participation and a partaker in the divine nature. The Word was indeed made human so that men might be made gods, and Christ showed us the Way. Even so, the Way requires a process of purification.

As Christians, we must embark upon the work of spiritual purification by accepting the Light of Christ and embracing the full power of God to bring about a spiritual transformation within us. To do so we must emulate the example of Jesus as well as the teachings of the Church's elders and saints.

Many pursue this at home, but the most ardent practitioners with yearning typically enter the priesthood or a monastic tradition. They follow an inner calling, and take upon themselves the role of the humble priest, monk or nun so they can devote themselves fully to the required effort of purgation. They are called by God to work fully at *theosis* by living a holy life while striving for living participation in the divine life. The target is a more perfect state of glorification, an inheritance that can never perish, spoil or fade. Such individuals need guidance for their efforts at returning back to incorruption.

Only when we actively work to become like Christ can we through that struggle achieve the ultimate blessing of divinization to experience Heaven while in this world. As Jesus is, man may be by relying on efforts of spiritual practice, the processes of purification, the doings of the Holy Spirit, God's breath of life, and Christ Himself to become even what He is. The Way is accomplished in Christ by growing to be more like Christ, and by assimilating his teachings into our way of life to shed what is errant and unwholesome for the higher.

Theosis is the promise of Christianity that all of us can achieve, which is to become glorified whilst alive so that we can experience the divine while living. As the Church Father Clement of Alexandria assured us, "he who obeys the Lord and follows the prophecy given through him ... becomes a god while still moving about in the flesh."

Thus, through Christian practice we can become one of the *twice born* that Jesus spoke of with Nicodemus. The entrance to a life in Christ can indeed transform us into *Homo Deus*, which is our independent purified sacred self whose attainment is the highest objective and deepest intent of the Christian path. The Church Father Athanasius of Alexandria said, "He was made human so that he might make us gods" and this is the ultimate purpose of Christianity. Many saints have achieved *theosis*, and left us their teachings to show us the Way.

We must firmly accept in the example of Jesus that "God became man so that man might become god." Many struggles you will face in the spiritual life while upon the road to *theosis*, but never forget that this is the ultimate purpose of Christianity.

The primary characteristic of the monastic life as well as the solitary path of spiritual struggles is that of *catharsis*. You engage in spiritual practice and various exercises to start purifying your body, mind and soul to achieve *theosis*, as many spiritual Fathers and saints in the past have done. It is through this transformational work at self-perfection that you prove, "Ye are gods" because you eventually will transcend the carnal attractions of the material world.

The spiritual life of a monastic is difficult because the work at becoming like Christ through divinization is a struggle. It is a process of progressive stages, accomplished through gradual degrees. Yet the pathway is there, and it is clear. The goal is reachable. Many have become saints through efforts that lead to spiritual union with God.

2 Corinthians 3:18 says, "We all, with unveiled face, beholding the glory of the Lord, are being transformed into the same image from one degree of glory to another." Gradual is the progress to glorification, but that target is worth our full efforts.

Jesus once said, "Truly, truly, I tell you, no one can see the Kingdom of Heaven unless he is born again." You are already born of semen and ova, and now you must be born of the Spirit through the process of divinization to become *Homo Deus*, which transcends your apparent self. This is how you become twice born and "sons of the highest."

This glorification or deification is a continuous flowing process whereby those who cultivate the Way will receive communion with the Holy Spirit. Over time through *catharsis* the practitioners will create glorified perfected souls, purified and Christ-like. The spiritual work of becoming like Christ through divinization lets one join the community of saints by also becoming a partaker in the divine nature and one of the sons of the highest. This is the spiritual pathway of Christianity.

The Christian spiritual path is therefore to become like what Jesus is Himself who "became man to deify us." In Christ man can achieve divinization, which is also called "deification," "glorification" or *theosis*, and man can then through this sanctification partake of the divine nature. The Church's version of salvation, or *theosis*, is a pathway of practice that restores God's original image in ourselves, which is why it is called glorification. The result is a heavenly attainment, a release from human mortality caused by the desires of the world.

Yes, "You are gods." You are an indwelling spirit encased within a physical shell. You are an unpurified soul or spirit yearning for an immaculate nature. Christ did indeed become incarnate by wearing the flesh so that you might learn how to become raised up and return back. The appropriate Christian spiritual path is to become like what Jesus is Himself who "became man to deify us."

This is the true spiritual pursuit within Christianity, and the Church offers a salvationist pathway of spiritual practice and transformation that is a road to this perfection of the body, mind and spirit.

For some it is the Christian monastic tradition or service of the priesthood, rather than just a holy life, that will enable them to more fully devote themselves to this pathway. Such deeper commitments to the spiritual life will usually be more effective at helping individuals cleanse their souls and may engender greater virtuous impulses. However, this route is not necessary for the solitary aspirant in the world who also endeavors with all his might to touch God's glory and achieve spiritualization. Nevertheless, the roads of monasticism and the clerical life offer options for those committed to sanctifying, purifying and regenerating their body, mind and spirit.

For the spiritual life we must always remember the true goal and use that perfect model as a beacon for guidance. Once again, it is as Saint Thomas Aquinas said, "The only-begotten Son of God, wanting to make us sharers in his divinity, assumed our nature, so that he, made man, might make men gods." As Athanasius also said, "The Word has been made human so that men might be made gods."

CHAPTER 2

THEOSIS, THEORIA AND *CATHARSIS* (*PURGATIO*)

Theosis is achieved through a process of transformation that occurs only if you devote yourself to deep spiritual training and practice. It is the holy result brought about by your personal efforts to purify your mind, your behavior and to tame your body according to the teachings of the Church. With *theosis* you will regain a purity of existence that doesn't fall into corruption, which can then partake more fully of the divine nature.

Anyone can achieve *theosis* who makes the effort, but it requires devoted spiritual work on your part as well as communion with the Holy Spirit. Your character must be washed again and again, and your spiritual efforts must also be sincere enough for Heaven to bless you with its grace.

Theosis is not just the quintessential purpose of Christian life, but the *very purpose* of human life. In other words, the purpose and goal of the Christian life – and especially of the clerical or monastic life totally dedicated to God - is actually that we attain *theosis* or "deification." To become a transfigured soul in union with God is called deification or divinization because it means attaining a purified "likeness to" or "union with" God that is the ultimate in spiritualization, a spiritual renewal depicted by the words, "Ye are gods." This being the case, the glorification of *theosis* is achievable only through a union between your cultivation efforts and God's uncreated energies, the operations of the Holy Spirit.

Washed again and again by the energies of the Holy Spirit in your body and mind, to attain *theosis* is to become one of the twice born, *Homo Deus*, who transcends the world while within it because you are in union with God and can transcend the restraining burdens of your physical body that pollutes your spiritual mentality.

Our saints have consistently taught to us that our personal work at cultivating the Christian life and Christian perfection is for the purpose of attaining *theosis,* or oneness with God. This will gradually produce a purification of our minds and behavior, called *catharsis*. This purification, together with the workings of the Holy Spirit felt inside you, will produce a growing experience of "illumination," called *theoria*, which will bring about a core transformation of your being prior to the attainment of true *theosis* spiritual union.

According to the standard formulation of this process, as described by Dionysius the Pseudo-Areopagite, there are three stages to the emergence of *theosis*:

- *Catharsis* or purification is the beginner's stage of purgation wherein you start turning away from all that is faulty, unclean or unwholesome in your mind and behavior. This is the foundational stage to *theosis*, and is characterized by activities that are the very heart of the Christian path. *Catharsis* constitutes ardent work at purifying your mind, body and behavior that we might call personal development work at rectification, self-correction, self-improvement or self-perfection. You must turn away from everything in your mind, body and behavior that is faulty and impure and shed all that is unwholesome in yourself, which is why this is called a process of purgation. During this foundational stage of *Purgatio* (*catharsis*), young priests, monks and nuns struggle through prayer and ascetic practices to cleanse themselves of impure thoughts, emotions, passions, and urges so that they can gain control of "their flesh" and its impure impulses. Specifically, they deny their ego and work at purging unwholesome patterns of anger and malice, pride, envy and jealousy, gluttony (that allows physical appetites to control you), sloth, greed (the desire for possessions), and the lust for sensual pleasures. This period of purgation, which often lasts many years, teaches aspirants how to triumph over many earthly desires and temptations, just as Christ had to resist temptation in the desert. Thus, those going through *catharsis* slowly cleanse themselves of character flaws, personality faults, undesirable behaviors and recurrent mental afflictions in order to gain control over the passions of their soul, their minds and their conduct. To assist in the process they must rely on devotion to God; absolute honesty in regular self-examination, self-reflection and confession; contemplative prayer; perseverance in the effort of gaining control over their will; obedience to their spiritual elders; and also the guidance of the Holy Spirit. The most important task is to purify their consciousness (*nous*), which is our faculty of knowledge (wisdom), discernment and behavior, so that their mind attains a state of quiet calm and clarity free of wayward thoughts and passions that might lead them down wayward paths. As a mind becomes purified, its spiritual understanding grows, passions subside and you finally become fit for a closer union with God.

- *Theoria* or illumination, is the second stage of the process to divinization whereby an aspirant's mind, body and behavior made pure – through adherence to regular prayer, meditation, contemplation, religious services, the routines laid out by the canon or Rule of one's tradition, and other spiritual practices – becomes blessed and transformed by the powers of the Holy Spirit. *Theoria* is a direct experience of God that you achieve in deep contemplation, and which transforms you through a communion of great stillness and peace. It is a type of illuminative experience other than thought that is "infused" with God's energies and acquired through your spiritual practices. Only those who cultivate purity of heart and dispassion, or control of the passions, can taste the experience of *theoria*, whose attainment requires much preparatory effort in spiritual practice. Despite the difficulties, the effort is worthwhile for it is the entire purpose of the spiritual life. It is a gift from the Holy Spirit to those who, through observance of God's commandments and devotion to spiritual practices, achieve a dispassionate attitude towards sensual indulgence and transcend their lower self in order to lift their minds to something higher. They practice mastering and transcending their personal desires, and practice self-denial of their own will to achieve the humility and ego-purity that God so loves. They learn to empty themselves of their own will and become entirely receptive to God's divine will, just as Jesus sacrificed his own will to the Father's for the redemption and salvation of all mankind. Teresa of Avila, author of *The Way of Perfection*, describes the means leading to the spiritual perfection of *theoria* as prayer, meditation, inner quiet, and repose of soul until one finally experiences this illuminative union with God, which she equates with rapture. Basically, it is through a gradual transformation caused by spiritual efforts that you finally achieve *theoria*, the experience of God through rapture or illumination, which happens to your whole person (soul or *nous*) rather than just your mind or body. During the illuminative experience, which is sometimes called the experience of uncreated light, you achieve a union with Heaven that silences all of your humanity. For the process of attaining and sustaining *theoria* the primary methods are active prayer, watchfulness over your thoughts, contemplation or meditation that involves indwelling in God, and a frequent inner active baptism by first your own efforts and then by the transformative energies of the Holy Spirit.

- Due to progress in the many types of intensified spiritual practices that produce and sustain *theoria*, an aspirant grows in quiet, illumination and grace until they finally achieve a perfect union with God called divinization, deification or glorification. Through your efforts at spiritual practice you become united to God by the grace of his energies, and the veil is then rent between earthly and heavenly matters. When in spiritual union, at this stage you can properly discern spiritual matters, and attain a holy wisdom like that of a saint such as knowing other people's thoughts or performing miraculous healing through the grace of God. This is the third stage of divinization, deification, glorification, sanctification, spiritualization, holiness or *theosis*, and it constitutes sainthood. This is the truest and highest achievement of the earthly Holy Life. It is the achievement of *Homo Deus*, being reborn by achieving a resplendent unity with God through his energies that will win you the kingdom of Heaven whilst alive.

By means of a *catharsis* of purification – of achieving a mind cleansed of wayward thoughts and passions, behavior purified of transgressions, and body washed by the Holy Spirit – a person comes to *theoria* and then to *theosis*. Then you become like what Jesus is Himself who "became man to deify us." This is the appropriate spiritual pursuit of a Christian, and the purpose of committing oneself to the holy life.

The "doer" in this process of deification is the Holy Spirit, with whom a human being joins his will to receive the necessary transforming grace. This blessed visitation is achieved through ardent prayer and other spiritual exercises, such as those commonly practiced by monastics, mendicants, friars, clerics or ascetics, until infrequent visits become a continuous presence. As Gregory Palamas teaches, the Christian saints and mystics became deified as they became filled with the Light (energy) of the Holy Spirit to the degree that they made themselves open to it by their devotion to spiritual practices. They become fully illuminated by the grace of God to the extent that they emptied their self-will, and thereby became sacred vessels of grace from which others could benefit in manifold ways.

The ultimate purpose of mankind is this mystical union with God. The ultimate pathway is the path of Christian perfection, which is something we must all pursue. It entails devotion to spiritual practices, the conquering of one's passions, the rectification of one's character and behavior, a commitment to modesty and humility, and the opening of oneself to the divine energies of the Holy Spirit. An individual can achieve this on his own, but it is easiest to pursue within a devoted spiritual life such as within a monastic community where you can out all your energies into the effort.

CHAPTER 3

THE COMMUNAL OR SOLITARY
PRACTICE ROAD TO *THEOSIS*

Once a person discovers Christ, they can begin the process that leads to *theosis*, which entails a gradual submission to God in order to become glorified. Naturally one must first pass through a stage of purification or purgation to prepare you for such an accomplishment.

The easiest way to *theosis* is to live in the community of the Church as a priest, friar, monk or nun. There you will be afforded the rare opportunity to pursue *theosis* under its care and protection, and can regularly partake of the sacraments while following the Rule of your tradition. The ecclesiastical communal life is entirely focused on finding God and servicing mankind, but you should only devote yourself to the cause if you have a conviction that this is the right decision for your life, and something that you truly want to do.

Monks usually live secluded contemplative lives while

friars live a communal life focused on finding God while remaining active in serving the community, so these two examples illustrate the simple fact that many options are available for the holy life. This book, although it applies to monks, friars, priests, ministers, reverends, abbots, ascetics, nuns and all spiritual others, will address *all* ecclesiastical personnel as if they were monks or nuns purely to simplify the discussion.

From the very beginning of the Church there were men and women who set out to lead lives dedicated to God each in his own way. Many of them, under the inspiration of the Holy Spirit, became hermits or founded religious families so that they could follow Christ in a special way that imitated him more closely. In their quest for the grace and divinity of God, their Rules typically revolved around a dedicated life of work, the study of canonical scripture, an intentional repetitive pattern of songful or silent prayer, and communal ritual. Some individuals chose the lives of becoming priests, ministers, friars, padres, monks or nuns as stated.

It is often difficult to choose the role for your life as well as the right tradition within the Church, and you must think carefully as to whether you can commit to the Rule, the full Offices, the practices and the community of a tradition that might attract you. One of the challenges of the monastic life whilst on this journey, perhaps the greatest, is not whether you can adhere to the discipline of the lifestyle but whether you can live with other men or women different from yourself and learn how to serve them. Therefore it is essential that you make such a decision of fellowship with the greatest care.

Although you may wish to wholly live a holy life, you

must also remember that everyone must work so that the community can maintain its upkeep. Fidelity to the observances of the work required by the community should not be considered a chore but a method to help transform you. The busyness of work lessens your leisure time and reduces casual interactions so that you can mentally focus on the spiritual life while at the same time experience a real world opportunity to test your spiritual attainments.

The central monastic belief is that a dedicated life of work (daily labor), the study of Scripture, contemplation, meditation, and constant (sometimes chant-filled) prayer will provide the structure of the journey toward an ideal of Christian perfection that will result in the emergence of a new spiritual life. Essentially, the monastic life for both men and women is dedicated toward an ideal that includes the attainment of *theosis*.

Within the holy life you must undertake the obligation to follow a rule of constant self-inspection and attendant devotion to self-improvement that is the essence of the process of purification or purgation. As a consequence of this commitment, the more intensified practices of prayer, contemplation, meditation, internal baptism, reading of the Scriptures, and other practices will more easily lead to *theoria* and then *theosis*.

The monastic life is a sacred journey of purgation that moves you toward a life of virtue. To achieve this, throughout your monastic life or other spiritual career, you must always police your thoughts and intentions and become continually mindful of your thinking and behavior. In what are they engaged? Since you should become observant enough to self-correct your thoughts and behavior all the time, this mindfulness or watchfulness should be considered basic daily practice that helps you to regulate your interior and exterior. Through the constant practice of being mindful of your thoughts, speech and behavior, and by a daily review of how you behaved during the day, you will gradually eliminate errant habit energies in your thoughts and behavior, cultivate more virtuous ways, attain control of your passions (which is necessary for *theoria*) and come ever closer to approximating the Christian life of excellence.

Over time, this continual work at correcting your shortcomings will bring about a true *conversion* - a "turning-around" of your life and transformation into a new way of existing in the world. By daily self-examination and review of your faults followed by confession, repentance, contrition and resolve, this will result in the emergence of a spiritual life centered around the internal virtues of modesty, humility and faith that will then regulate your behavior while inviting into yourself the energies of the Holy Spirit. Basically, the acts of repentance and contrition that spur one into becoming a better person are the chief works of a monk or nun. They are a means of becoming humble of heart as well as pure and spotless before God.

Having a clear mind gives power to one's efforts at self-correction, and therefore silent meditation, since it is well-known to produce greater mental clarity, must be another of your required daily practices. It is another type of humility practice where you give up your ego and empty yourself of yourself whereupon you can more readily experience the fullness of God through inner silence. Normally we are engaged in endless analysis about things, mentally tossing over things here and there while also criticizing ourselves, scorning others and passing judgment on all sorts of issues with an endlessly running internal dialogue. We might even eat our meals in silence, but usually our mind is still spinning here and there with inner self-talk filled with defilements. Meditation practice will help decrease this tendency of wandering thoughts and negative narrative over time.

Silence that is operative in the environment, and which gradually develops within your own mind due to spiritual practices, is critical to a monk's or nun's development. It is more than a state of reverence assumed by participants prior to something happening. By daily practice of indwelling in God where you give up your own thoughts and will, you allow God to come into you and take their place. By so doing you will gradually achieve an inner silence, peace, and serenity that characterizes the holy life, and which can blossom into spiritual gifts such as the illuminative stage of *theoria*.

Prayer is another necessary daily practice. It is considered that no one can reach *theosis* without impeccable Christian living, which you attain through the practice of mindfulness or watchfulness to improve your behavior, yet pure living must also be accompanied by regular faithful prayer. When praying you must say the words distinctly, observe the pauses and never hurry. You must keep your mind on the prayer without becoming distracted. Many monastic traditions, in their quest for the grace and divinity of God, have adopted the repetitive prayer pattern of the desert Christian Fathers, such as the "Prayer of the Heart." The Prayer of the Heart is a prayer that never ceases, just as Paul exhorts us in 1 Thessalonians 5:17 ("Pray without ceasing"). This unceasing prayer of the heart is a dominant theme in the writings of the saints and Church Fathers, especially those accounts collected in the *Philokalia*, because it is a stage of transformation leading to *theoria*.

Another of your daily practices might be devotional singing or chanting. With chant-filled prayer you should chant with the greatest devotion that arouses deep spiritual emotions while also feeling the transformational power of the sounds. The power of the chanting should stimulate and then harmonize your internal energy. The practice of chanting hymns and singing spiritual songs should never be monotonous because the sound power should vibrate the energy within you at different parts of your body, or your whole body at once, and then the practice becomes the most effective.

Another of your daily practices should be inner purification that involves your internal energy once again as in chanting. This is a daily ablution of inner baptism that uses your breathing or vital life energy to internally wash and consecrate your physical body to God. By washing ourselves using the vital energy breathed into us by God, by which we became living creatures, we can consecrate our interiors and more readily beckon *catharsis*, *theoria*, *theosis* and the attainment of *Homo Deus*.

Another daily practice should be a contemplative, prayerful reading of the Scriptures, such as done in *Lectio Divina*. Here you read a scriptural passage, reflect upon the meaning, and then enter into an inner silence to await any other inspirations as to its message.

A final part of your necessary daily practices must include physical exercises to maintain your health and fitness, for it is very easy for monks and nuns and priests, although they may be advanced in spiritual discipline, to neglect their bodies or even subject themselves to ascetic extremes that might weaken or harm their bodies. The maintenance of your physical health through regular diet and exercise is better than remedy or cure, but this common sense is neglected in most spiritual occupations.

Fidelity to these practices transforms a person. *Theoria* is achieved through the combination of these practices that comprise the stage of *catharsis* or purgation, which is the initiatory phase of the process to *theosis*. As a monk or nun grows in holiness and grace from their daily spiritual efforts, God will often bless them with reminders of the Holy Spirit.

While in the monastic tradition physical labor helps us to maintain our strength and fitness, once again it must be emphasized that everyone should also participate in physical exercises that will perfect their body, just as they must work on perfecting their ways of thinking and doing as they strive to achieve a state of incorruption. For this objective of exercise we should rely upon the very best methods discovered in the world for spiritual aspirants, which are the practices of yoga and the martial arts.

These are powerful antidotes used in many traditions to stave off the inevitability of physical decline, and which will also move your inner vital energy in tune with the Holy Spirit. With health, it becomes easier for the blessings of the Holy Spirit to penetrate your being to bring about *theosis* and *theoria*, a joining with God. This is why all priests, monks and nuns should take up a daily exercise regime.

CHAPTER 4

MEDITATION PRACTICE
TO ATTAIN *THEORIA*

One of your daily practices must be meditation, a time of sacred quietude where you abandon the thoughts and worries normally dominating your mind, which always bind it to material things, and through that emptying allow God to fill you instead.

This is how you experience God in *theoria*, which is a type of internal illumination where you retain the conscious capability of *knowing* but your human thought-stream empties while the presence of God predominates. It is a state characterized by great internal peace where our coarse conceptual faculties are quieted, thus producing inner silence and a serene composure of the soul, but there is also a type of bliss and spirit you feel from being enveloped by the presence of God. Your mind seems empty of thoughts but your awareness still shines and you feel a subtle sense of holy fullness inside you.

Meditation practice is therefore a type of internal quiet time where you practice abandoning your personal thought concerns and mental reflections so that you can instead let God predominate in their place. It is a practice of mental quiet that can, in time, come to sustain you.

During meditation there is a greater union or coupling with God because you silence the doings of your ego that normally push Him away, and now you let God predominate because you abolish the mental activity that would normally silence His presence. It is a time of being alone with just Him, and it is made possible because you silence your egotistic demands that normally get in the way. The Bible therefore instructs us:

- Be still and know that I am God (Ps 46:10)
- Be still before the Lord and wait patiently for Him (Ps 37:7)
- For God alone my soul waits in silence; from Him comes my salvation. (Ps 62:1)
- But I stilled and quieted my soul; like a weaned child with its mother, like a weaned child is my soul within me. (Ps 131:2)
- Tremble and do not sin; when you are on your beds, search your hearts and be silent. (Ps 4:4)

Some traditions call this quiet emptying of thoughts "contemplation" because the original word for *theoria* was *contemplatio*, the highest mental activity of mankind where there are no deliberations, complexities, nor fabrications stirring within the mind. In *contemplatio* or *theoria* there is just blazing awareness without the busyness of the noisy intellect we normally hear speaking inside our heads. The mind becomes "empty" but there is still the knowing of objects and life. The common term for practicing this in today's world is "meditation" whereas "contemplation" is the vocabulary we now employ for a type of pondering, analysis or thinking over a topic where you are deeply involved with thoughts and conceptions.

In contemplation your thinking powers are exerted, but during meditation practice you try to abandon your thought-stream and thought processes. Because during meditation you don't identify with your inner narrative but just watch your thoughts with a heightened awareness, they will gradually die down due to the lack of injected energy, your mental narrating stream of self-talk will lessen, and your mental realm will become quiet and clear. When you give away your egocentric mental activity, and consequentially experience mental peace because you give all your concerns over to God at this time, then because of that humility you become will more peaceful and receptive to God's energies. In that state where your ego is ignored, you can start to fill with a greater degree of God's presence and inspiration.

Now, since some traditions consider the meaning of meditation and contemplation reversed, this is just a difference in vocabulary. By no means does this invalidate the methods for how to contemplate a topic or engage in thought-less meditation.

Although contemplation rightly means thinking, the highest form of contemplation is a form of "having no thoughts" because you look directly at God without thinking and just remain in that presence. A direct vision or experience of God is beyond conceptual knowledge, so it is by the practice of meditation, where you practice abandoning your thoughts and remaining detached from them when they arise, that you purify yourself and prepare for a greater experience of quiet holiness. Since this is why we enter into the holy life, it is essential that meditation should become part of your daily spiritual practice.

As our ordinary knowledge is based on contemplative or discursive thinking, and because *gnosis* is not only limited but can become a barrier between man and God, we therefore need to abandon conceptual thinking during meditation practice so that we might better experience God during this period of surrender. By emptying ourselves of attachments to *nous,* the mind of intellect and will, through this surrendering practice of humility you will start to more fully experience God's holy presence just as Elijah only experienced God's presence after he ignored the loud distractions of the earthquake, wind and fire in the desert. Similarly, once you also start to abandon the internal distractions that are always occupying your mind, you will begin to sense the presence of God to a much greater degree. Mental silence is an opportunity to *listen* to divine inspirations without your own thoughts getting in the way. The Holy Spirit will often bring sacred thoughts to a man's mind and this is how to hear them.

Every day you must practice meditation. Through meditation practice you will gradually gain a strong and dependable internal peace by emptying your mind of attractions to every passion and desire and then they will die down. When you learn how to let go of personal desires so that they no longer exert control over you, they will stop preoccupying your consciousness and free your mind so that it lives in a state of heightened purity. Letting go of self-concerns during meditation practice allows your mind to fill with God's presence in their place. This freedom from self-concerns is like a great burden being lifted off your shoulders, and your mind will experience a great purity and bliss to the degree that you master self-abandonment.

You should practice this not just via meditation, but should prepare for it by watching your mind during ordinary affairs so that you might, every moment, cut off your errant tendencies and mental fixations. You want to both correct your behavior through watchfulness and also gain control of your senses so that you don't become fused with passionate desires but simply let them flow through you. Due to a constant mindfulness that with detachment sees things independently and clearly as if they were images within a mirror, the busyness of your mental facilities will gradually fade and an inner quiet will assume their place.

This internal peace is one of the goals of Christianity, and is the fruit or reward of the Christian life. Just as Jesus sacrificed himself for our redemption and salvation, during meditation you should practice a sacrificial self-denial of your own will by ignoring desires so that they pass over you and naturally die away. You accomplish this ability, and progressively gain an independence where they lose their hold on you, by practicing detachment rather than forceful suppression. You should practice detaching from the objects of your mind so that you can ignore them, and use reasoning about the benefits of ignoring them when detachment becomes too difficult.

In true humility you don't suppress your will, but become humble through forsaking yourself by offering your willfulness away. This offering can be considered a type of charity, and thus a "good deed" within Christianity. It is by the "self-emptying" of Jesus's own will that He became wholly receptive to God's divine will, which is the example we must emulate. By "emptying yourself" you will fill with divine grace, for it will rush in to fill the void you create when you humbly open yourself to the divine.

This humility achieved through meditation practice, where during that time you offer away your will and your thoughts, results in mystical union with God - *theoria*. To experience *theoria* you must train to sever your mental attachments to all worldly concerns, all earthly pleasures, and by learning how to transcend the world you will over time come closer to God.

This is the attainment achieved by our spiritual Fathers and the saints of our tradition. A meditative life or contemplative life is a life devoted to God in this manner where every day we empty ourselves of ego and pride and become more obedient to His will rather than our own will that is centered around selfish impulses and indulgences.

According to John of the Cross, this "self-emptying" of our own will to become entirely receptive to God and the divine will is *kenosis*. When you practice obedience to God then this humility invites His presence (because you silence your own will and abandoning occupying yourself with the passions) and becomes God's way of transforming you.

There are a variety of Christian meditation practices, often called contemplation practices, which instruct you to "look at," "gaze at," or "be aware of" God and the Divine. By patiently "indwelling in God" rather than in your own thoughts, you will slowly achieve an inner peace and serene quietude absent of thoughts that fills you with God's energies. Through such practice you will also gradually learn how to remain undistracted by the mind's inner movements and by events outside of the mind.

Meditation is thus a form of *pure prayer* to God that is free of thoughts; contains no mental forms, shapes or images; does not introduce any outside elements; and is full only of God, His powers, and His will rather than your own. It is a mental solitude of being free from all personal mental efforts such as self-talk, and is an offering up of yourself to tranquility instead.

When you practice meditation it should be just as when you practice centering prayer and give your thoughts and will over to God, holding nothing as your own, and trusting that He will handle everything. For instance, monks who enter a monastery give up all their possessions so that they don't need to be concerned with material concerns, and now they take a step further by giving up even their own thoughts and will.

Through the practice of daily meditation you will gradually cleanse your spirit, which is the purer, more internal and truer element of human existence. Meditation enables you to transcend everything that you consider yourself and enter the infinite space of God that is limitless. The spirit of God is the spirit of peace, and this is what you touch through meditation practice. This is the one spiritual practice most fitting to the human person.

An individual becomes a monk or nun because they want to cast aside every element, external or internal, that impedes their relationship with God since those things create a barrier between themselves and God's presence in their life. If one is brimming full of their own thoughts and desires, or personal passions and vexations, there is little room for God to enter. Thoughts unite our self to something other than God, as in idolatry, and clinging to them is the same as occupying your heart by another god other than God. Hence, through the daily practice of emptying yourself through meditation practice, and giving all your thoughts, desires and concerns over to God at that time, you will create for those moments the opportunity for God to come more fully into your life.

The pure mind - a mind empty of negative self-talk, wandering thoughts, mental afflictions, and self-centered concerns - attracts God to itself. Withdrawing one's mind from the images of the world during meditation time is therefore one of the purgative methods of spiritual practice. To remain in this state without distraction or disturbance eventually enables you to achieve a closer spiritual union with God, or *theoria*. During *theoria* your mind still shines with awareness because you are not asleep, which is why it is also termed "illumination." However, the loudness of your thoughts has subsided so that your mind seems like a clear sky empty in all directions, which is also the meaning of being "illuminated." In that state, which seems empty of self-centeredness, you will feel the fullness of the presence of God.

A "contemplative life" is a life devoted to God through this sort of practice rather than preoccupied with extraordinary thinking activities.

Meditation is practiced to achieve an aloneness with God where you can become one with God and God only rather than remain preoccupied by your own thoughts and concerns. It is a state of surrendering, poverty and humility because to achieve this you must empty yourself of your own will and detach yourself from your own personal concerns to become entirely receptive to God's divine presence filling you in their place. By "emptying yourself" you will fill with divine grace, becoming slowly transformed into "the likeness of Christ." Nothing else will unite you to God as much as this. This union with God is possible, for the saints of the Church serve as witnesses.

Practicing in this way, untying your mind from earthly things for a certain period every day, gradually you will start to share in the divine energies - those of the Father, the Holy Spirit and Son who has taken this path before you. You will produce a mode for the Holy Spirit to act within you Who will transform you from within, helping to wash away personality flaws just as a river washes away muddy pollution. In its place you will be left with a mental peace, clarity and purity like nothing previously known. The transformative energies you will experience will be God's response to your efforts, and will be like a "spring of water that wells up to eternal life."

The person who meditates through this fasting of thoughts, and who prays and rectifies their behavior, will certainly begin the process of divinization that restores you to the perfect image of God. They will become glorified because the spirit of God will move within them and transform them. In a certain way they will become absorbed by God, and thus become in tune with His perfection as was Christ.

Meditation, where you let go of your thoughts, is thus a type of communing time with God. This is the only thing in life worth your time and effort. It is not a type of intellectual contemplation or period of heavy thinking and reflection but a time of unknowingness where you are uninvolved with (detached from your) conceptual processes but simply know what appears within your consciousness without overly identifying with it. Thoughts will then slowly recede in volume and your mind will become much quieter and peaceful. There is the greatest of value in touching this quiet for this is when you can approach God most closely.

The Uncreated cannot be grasped by the rational mind, so meditation practice is a time where you empty yourself of yourself so that you can attain harmony with the Uncreated. This is how you achieve the experiential union of *theoria* that is the target of the religious life. Your discursive reasoning is not obliterated but surrendered to God through a natural freedom and openness that doesn't suppress mental activity, for the mind should always be permitted to give birth to thoughts.

The way to prepare for *theoria* is by practicing meditation. You, during meditation time, practice giving up yourself completely, or practice simply watching your thoughts and being aware of your mind's contents without becoming so involved with them that you lose your sense of presence. By watching thoughts with an independent sense of detachment, and by not providing distractions with energy by identifying with them or following them, your tendency to meander in thoughts will die down and your thought-stream will become quiet. Then in that silence, waiting on God without expectations, the inner light can grow.

In Phil 2:7 it is said that Jesus "emptied himself," which speaks to the very same procedure. All Christians should aspire to have an actual direct experience of God in this same way, which is by *theoria* attained through meditation practice (that abandons thoughts) and other spiritual exercises.

It is not that you should cultivate an inner quiet where you try to think of God's attributes, for God is essentially unfathomable, incomprehensible, and unthinkable in terms of thoughts or images. God transcends every thought so you must abandon thoughts to experience God. To achieve *theoria,* you must abandon all thoughts or images of His qualities, as well as thoughts of your self and self-concerns, because He is perfectly pure. Then your mind will become in harmony with His unfathomable being. That is how you achieve spiritual union with God by inviting Him into your presence. It is through a mental purity empty of thoughts that you establish such a holy communion. This is why you should try to give all your thoughts and problems over to God, dropping all your concerns, when you seek deep communion during meditation time. Similarly, Teresa of Avila said that daily prayers should also revolve around "giving myself totally to the Lord" where you offer yourself away like this.

God is without mark or sign or stain, and because of that purity no human mind can touch His perfect nature through thoughts, so you must try to abandon thoughts during a time of meditation to achieve a greater closeness. The best analogy is to free your mind of all fabrications so that it becomes empty like vast formless space, which is insubstantial and free of all things. That is why we say that a meditative mind is a mind without attributes. In other words, imagine that you become a vast empty space free of a body and thoughts, and remain waitful in that state but without the expectation of waiting. One can come to know God better in such a state.

The barrier to God is not just our behavior but the fact

that our mind is constantly afflicted with distractions, annoyances and agitations. It wanders here and there commenting on and judging everything. It is continually cut to pieces by various thoughts, passions, desires and other foreign elements that go against its inherently pure nature. Meditation is a chance to restore wholeness to our mind, a time to stop cutting it into pieces by untying it from material attachments, and thereby returning to an experience of God so full that it envelops our being and silences our personality. During meditation practice, therefore, you must undertake a surrender like Christ in completely giving up your own thinking and will to the Father. During meditation you must give thoughts away and surrender yourself to God completely.

CONTEMPLATION

We can only discover through the human mind the various energies and attributes of God, but in taking His purity as the sole content of our minds during meditation we at that time become more like His perfect essence. It is a time when by giving up our own thoughts we can become washed by His glory and a little bit more purified.

Nevertheless there is call for us to also think about things too. We definitely should also practice conceptual deliberations or contemplations over matters, for that is the purpose of the consciousness we have been given. Our mind is not to be thwarted in its functioning, but simply rested on a regular basis. As Philippians 4:8 instructs, "Finally, brothers and sisters, whatever is true, whatever is noble, whatever is right, whatever is pure, whatever is lovely, whatever is admirable - if anything is excellent or praiseworthy - think about such things."

As an alternative to formless meditations where you empty your thoughts completely, you can therefore practice the opposite sort of contemplation where you fill your *nous* or soul with the glories of God such as the thoughts and feelings of boundless love, joy or compassion that are so great that the experience fills every part of your being and spreads out into the entire universe.

In this type of useful contemplation practice, you should fill your mind and body with the energy of an infinite, boundless, immeasurable emotion that has no limiting borders, and should remain in that state for as long as possible without any other thoughts interceding. This is also a form of very useful spiritual contemplation practice.

You should make a regular practice of this type of contemplation using the subjects of infinite joy, infinite love, infinite compassion, infinite kindness, infinite giving, infinite benevolence, infinite mercy, infinite humility, infinite courage, infinite glory, infinite exaltation, infinite light and infinite peace. Any contemplation you practice should so monopolize your consciousness by being felt so deeply that even the energy of your body feels permeated by that infinite contemplation. These contemplations are like the purified powers of God Himself and through deep absorption will wash your soul with their influence.

You can also meditate on infinite omnipresence, which is the infinite extension of empty space in all directions that encompasses all things, just as does God's existence. This state of physical and mental fullness, which should admit no other thoughts, will help free you from your attachment to coarse thoughts and the material world of being.

In such contemplations you don't abandon thoughts as in meditation practice but hold onto a big thought feeling that involves the whole you, that becomes the whole you, and is infinite in size without borders or limits. Sometimes you will feel the energy of your body becoming washed and transformed by such contemplations, which will help to purify your personality because the more you think and act a certain way the more you will naturally become that way. This is why they should be practiced.

Abba Anthony said, "Whoever hammers a lump of iron, first decides what he is going to make of it, a scythe, a sword, or an axe. Even so we ought to make up our minds what kind of virtue we want to forge or we labor in vain." He reminds us to pick those virtues we wish in our character, and then you must practice becoming that virtue in an infinite way during meditation, regularly practice this contemplation, consistently act that way in real life, and then it will truly become incorporated into our psyche.

Following Christ's instruction to "go into your room or closet and shut the door and pray to your father who is in secret" (Matthew 6:6), you can also use quiet times to talk to God as if in a conversation asking for help in becoming this way, or can focus your mind like this and impress your personality with such absorptions. At those times you must detach from all other concerns and envelop yourself fully in these immeasurable contemplations that involve tremendously immense feelings that permeate you and transform your being.

Monastic practice has as one of its major purposes the task of purifying your soul, and both meditation and contemplation that empty thoughts or concentrate on one virtuous large super-thought are means to do so. Those who practice meditation and contemplation in this way regularly find them personally meaningful and spiritually significant. They are a method of spiritual transformation.

Over time your practice of the Sacred Quietude of meditation will help to silence pride and self-importance, heighten your mental clarity, and help you to work at eliminating your faults and imperfections. The practice of contemplating Infinite Qualities will help you develop personal virtues as well. Together these practices will help you attain a more stable internal peace and mental clarity that will often cause you to feel *fully alive* as if you were a vivid living presence. This is the bliss that God grants us.

This is the beginning of *theoria* or unity with God. After much practice and experience with illumination or *theoria*, a humble aspirant will start achieving the divine union of *theosis*, and will start to properly discern many spiritual matters, which is developing holy wisdom.

CHAPTER 5

MASTERING YOURSELF REQUIRES CONTINUAL CORRECTION OF YOUR MIND AND BEHAVIOR

Many individuals are devoted to some aspect of helping the world through various charitable or philanthropic efforts. However, saving the world or just saving yourself ultimately starts with private personal efforts at correcting your own thoughts and behavior. In fact, spiritual maturity also demands self-rectification of your mind and behavior. Once you have started rectifying yourself and achieve some degree of self-mastery and purity, only then do you really become qualified to help others.

Christianity has world salvation as its primary mission because as we work to become better people we will eventually accumulate into a force great enough to better the world. The goal of Christian perfection therefore requires that we work hard to eliminate our character flaws, faults, our vices and bad habits so that we become more effective. We must work at their reduction and adopt positive virtues in their place. This is a process which necessitates that we concentrate on the within.

Christian perfection requires an alert attentiveness over your thinking and behavior so that you do not stray from propriety or righteousness, and asks that you always correct yourself whenever you catch yourself succumbing to faulty ways. In essence, the Christian path requires you to master your mind and behavior to become a better person. The objective is to become your highest best self.

One reason that society is blessed with peacefulness and social well-being is because we have laws. Laws do not always dissuade people from errant behaviors, however, so the real reason that peace and harmony have come to dominate society is because religions have also stressed principles of good behavior, ethics and morality, and virtue and values. For us on the Christian path, the first step to learning virtue and good conduct is to keep the Ten Commandments, but there are other virtues and values we should also cultivate, and vices to avoid.

Those in the consecrated life should have Christian perfection as their goal where one grows to become more like Christ over time. To accomplish this you must do all that you can to live as Christ lived, according to the teachings and example of Christ. There is a method of self-correction that makes this possible, and which has long been a mainstay of the Christian monastic tradition. It is a method where you learn to separate yourself from your passions and purify your thoughts and behavior. Through this process of sanctification you can attain purity and become holy.

Through slow and gradual steps you can purify your thoughts and behavior to become more like Christ and achieve *theosis* as He did. Meditation and prayer are part of this process, but the critical key is the practice of keeping tabs on your behavior and striving to improve it. This requires a bit of introspection and self-policing, but everyone can practice this technique. When you catch yourself doing something wrong or thinking something wrong you should stop it at that moment, but stopping requires strong awareness and will. Nevertheless, this is the basis of all self-improvement practices. Without self-correction efforts all of us will remain trapped in recurrent loops of bad behavior, for as Paul said, "I do not do the good I want, but the evil I do not want to do is what I do – this I keep on doing" (Romans 7:19).

This technique of watchful self-correction requires maintaining a sense of presence where you are self-observant, self-aware and a bit detached from what you are doing rather than fully entrained with some activity where you lose your objectivity entirely. In other words, you always need to be watching yourself – your mind and behavior – with an awareness like that of a spectator who from that independent perspective objectively sees what you are doing and what is actually going on. It requires a presence or clarity of mind to achieve this sort of self-observation, but this is a characteristic that you can and do gradually cultivate through meditation practice. Once you start meditating, your mind will also become clearer and more observant to help in this task because it will start to rid itself of unnecessary mental clutter that usually preoccupies it as distractions.

You will start becoming kinder, more empathetic and

more concerned about other people and their feelings once you start using this daily technique of self-purification. Gentleness, which encompasses forgiveness, acceptance and love, starts developing to a greater force within you as you start becoming aware of what you are doing and more concerned about other people and their feelings, needs or troubles.

This means of self-perfection is to practice constant awareness of your mind-stream, and subsequently correct your mental and physical behavior as you observe it. If you find yourself harboring ill will or malice, anger, selfishness, unkind thoughts or improper thoughts, you should try to cut them off in that instant. In the evening you should review those efforts and confess those struggles to God, and asking for God's help to change any errant aspects of your personality you have discovered.

You ultimately want to lighten the darker aspects of your character through this method of self-correction. However, this can only happen through an awareness of wrongs you commit, and then work at self-correction. Therefore you must train to always look within and evaluate your own behavior to see if you are making progress at becoming a better person. When you can change errant personality traits you don't like about yourself then you actually become master of yourself. However, to accomplish this you might have to ask for God's assistance. The monastic life provides you with an environment where you can easily practice this daily routine and gradually accomplish self-improvement over time.

To become aware of your missteps through self-observation and reflection is called the "examination of conscience." It is a method taught by Saint Ignatius of Loyola in his *Spiritual Exercises,* and is based on the teachings of the Apostle Paul that we can maintain a clear conscience by doing what is right rather than wrong. The basic method of self-correction for accomplishing this is as follows:

- You always watch your thoughts and behavior with mindful attention throughout the day so that you know what you are actually thinking and how you are behaving. You must start to cultivate a continual watchfulness of whatever you are thinking, saying and doing, but your personality should remain soft and humble throughout this practice rather than become hard and unforgiving.

- Immediately correct any errors in your wayward thoughts, emotions, and behaviors whenever you notice them. This requires both awareness and willpower for it is hard to break the momentum of our thoughts or actions. It requires courage, determination and strength of will to break free from the momentum of inclinations but in that moment you become master of yourself rather than a slave to errant dispositions. You could also say that it requires humility to be able to detach from passions or habit energies rather than to automatically follow them. The objective is to stop clinging to errant thinking and behavior whenever discovered, and to replace them with something more wholesome. This requires that you gradually free yourself from errant thinking habits, errant perspectives and longstanding habits that are a source of power over you. Through this practice of immediate self-correction you will start freeing yourself from slavery to your ingrained patterns of doing and thinking. You will thereby develop a new spiritual way of being. Self-correcting yourself requires a devotion to rectitude that is opposed to imperfections. However, through the practice of correcting yourself you are learning to become like Christ because you are becoming obedient to Christ's image in yourself – an image that knows right from wrong. When awareness calls note, you must therefore cut off your wrong thoughts or conduct, however difficult, and demonstrate your highest best self at that moment. The goal is to always express noble consummate behavior. Your errant thoughts and behaviors that can be cut off, cut off; those that can be ignored, ignore; those that can be transformed, transform into the best and highest; those errant tendencies that have not arisen do not let them arise. For help in changing your habits, two books that can help a lot are *The Power of Habit* (Charles Duhigg) and *Atomic Habits* (James Clear).

- On a card you always carry with you, or in a small diary you hang at your side, you should record your thought or behavioral infractions when noticed. Alternatively, you can also remember them at the end of the day by performing a daily review. You may also follow the method of Benjamin Franklin in his autobiography (for developing thirteen virtues to build his character by policing his behavior throughout the day), or that of Yuan Liao Fan in *Liao-Fan's Four Lessons* that over the centuries has taught countless people how to engage in self-correction.

- Looking back in a review of your day, in an attitude of prayer and thankfulness for being given an opportunity to reduce your faults, scrutinize your day's behavior before retiring. This is a time to examine the day's events and unearth your reasons for doing what you did. Developing an understanding of your behavior is the most important part to this process. You must examine whatever you did, differencing between right and wrong, and question the motives behind what you consider faults or blemishes so that you can learn how to change your heart and procedures. Basically, you must uncover your motivations for any harm or slights you have committed. During this daily review, reflect upon whether anger, resentment, ill will, greed, lust or other egoistic attachments played a role in your transgressions against propriety. Consider how you should have instead behaved during the day and analyze how to change your conduct. After analyzing your weaknesses, derive a plan for reform so that deficiencies are not repeated, which is essentially a plan for progressing in rectitude and purity. Then *commit* to instituting those alterations and vow to behave in the future in line with a more perfect ideal. The goal is to transform your present personality and thereby ascend spiritually rather than simply strive to avoid sins and errors.

- In consideration of your transgressions during the day and with Christ as the model, imagine in your mind being an ideal representative of the corrected, perfected way you aspire to become. Hold that image within your mind and regularly bring it up as the model of perfection you are working towards. You must aim to eliminate blemishes in your character and behavior that you discover through each new day's review using your ideal vision as a guide. Once again, you are encouraged to read *The Autobiography of Benjamin Franklin* and *Liao-Fan's Four Lessons* because they can teach you how to successfully make this effort. Another book related to this task is Frank Bettger's *How I Raised Myself From Failure to Success in Selling*.

• Lastly, confess your errors to Heaven, showing sincere remorse, renew a vow that you are committed to change yourself according to God's more perfect design, and ask for Heaven's help in the forward endeavor to eliminate your personality flaws, faults and mistakes. Pray to God asking for help in amending your ways, and go to sleep knowing that all wrongs can be righted and a new beginning is tomorrow.

Over time, through this simple process of self-observation and self-policing where you immediately correct your faults when noticed and review your work at the end of the day, you will begin to permanently eliminate errors in your mental habits and conduct, and correct various stains on your soul. Gradually, you will see what a great difference and blessing this method brings to you. As you take pains to reform yourself of failings, all sorts of circumstances will gradually get better for you.

By practicing mindfulness and introspection so that you begin to truly notice what is being thought in your own mind and why, you will also come to recognize what usually influences you almost subliminally without your recognition. Through that heightened awareness you will then start to be able to correct wrong inclinations with a spirit of nobility. What you whisper to yourself has a great influence on the direction of your thoughts and actions, as well as your ethics and morality. When you start looking at what you are truly thinking instead of blindly just doing things, then you can start improving all your interactions with others.

This process of virtue training is based on cultivating a simple and permanent attentiveness that always focuses on the condition of your heart and mind. Are you acting out of your best self or letting negative thoughts control you? Are you putting others before yourself or yourself before others? Are you working to better yourself and the others around you or just engaging in selfish impulses?

By shining your inward light on your outward actions and inner intentions, your inner light becomes your teacher. As Saint Bernard said, this type of attention "regulates the affections, directs the actions, and corrects defects." By mindfully watching yourself you will end up performing more acts of humility, love and self-sacrifice, which is how this method transforms your behavior.

Examining your conscience in real time and at the day's end in review is a most important spiritual exercise. Christian perfection is the aim to achieve spiritual maturity, and this watchfulness is the reliable method that achieves it. It will at first be a struggle to maintain this practice but it will soon become habitual and then natural. It should become a rule of self-management for your whole life that will tremendously impact your behavior for the better.

Although difficult at the start to the extent that it might even seem like spiritual warfare, as time goes your diary of self-correction will be filled by less and less daily errors. You will also feel inside you a sense of growing spiritual renewal, comfort, cleanliness and strength. You will feel that you are on the right path because you are getting better in every way. But be patient and yet persistent. Take heart in the fact that no one can change everything over night in one stroke.

In time, through this habitual practice you will also learn not to react with mental violence or emotional aggressiveness in response to things and events taking place around you. Instead, you will treat them with greater detachment, patience and acceptance, and become better able to flow from experience to experience without emotional difficulties. As you learn to correct yourself, you will less frequently project impassioned or errant concepts onto situations or people, or interpret them harshly, but will respond with a greater sense of understanding, tolerance and acceptance that is the heart of love.

Your thinking will therefore become more careful and your social skills will also heighten. Your personality will soften, your manners will improve and you'll become more open-minded and accepting of others while recognizing their own problems in overcoming personal failings. Basically, you will begin to take back control of your emotional mind and begin to reform your habits.

What are habits? They are things we have learned to do as a result of our previous conditioning, and which have become our normal way of behaving. They are not natural, however, because we weren't born with any of them. They are programs that stuck but they can be replaced with new and better behaviors. This method helps you change them.

This daily practice of mindfulness, rectification and

renewal is the basis of a consecrated life that seeks sanctification, purification and perfection in manifesting the virtues. These are the purposes of the monastic tradition and this is the process that draws one closer to God because *this is the path of purification* leading to *theoria* and *theosis*. This *is* the process that makes a person worthy to see God.

One must strive to live a holy life to become truly holy. This is the way, which is a way of pain, disappointment and struggle. Through the formal routines of your tradition along with meditation, prayer and this practice of self-correction, this totality of spiritual efforts will evolve into fulfillment. This cleansing will make it possible for you to experience a closer union with God and will invite into you the energies of the Holy Spirit.

The supreme goal is to have the mind of Christ as you walk, and this daily practice is the very instrument of that goal. The major problem is our passions, which are preoccupations or movements of our soul contrary to its pure nature. This method helps us gradually purify our emotions, passions and desires so they don't control us. When you abandon the blemish of continually falling into lusts and desires you will begin to live with a purity of consciousness as God intended, and start living the life of your essence as God made you.

"Holiness" in sacred writings is a habitual disposition of the soul. It is arrived at through purification efforts just like this. Holiness, sanctification, saintliness or Christian perfection are all characteristics of *theosis*, and this level of spiritualization implies being cleansed from sin. It implies you have been reforming yourself of faults and non-virtuous tendencies. This technique gives you a sure method of self-reform where you can work at recognizing and then correcting your own faults and vices after you finally see what they are.

The standards for being a good person have been generally the same throughout the centuries, so through this process of blunting your sharp edges, eliminating your imperfections and polishing your virtues you can indeed start to experience the process of glorification.

Remember that through this practice you won't just purify yourself of errors but can become endowed with more virtues. 2 Peter 1:5-7 admonishes us: "... make every effort to add to your faith goodness; and to goodness, knowledge; and to knowledge, self-control; and to self-control, perseverance; and to perseverance, godliness; and to godliness, mutual affection; and to mutual affection, love." In Mark 12:31 we are told to love others as yourself, which means working for their welfare, which actually produces the feeling of brotherhood and family. We can use mindfulness to cultivate such virtues.

One can use this very technique to not only seek moral excellence and remove the abrasive qualities of our personalities, but as per the famous examples in *The Autobiography of Benjamin Franklin* and *Liao Fan's Four Lessons*, we can use self-observation to develop deeper virtues that are normally considered the fruits of the Holy Spirit. Any impetus to develop deeper virtues, however, will require work on our part. We cannot just meditate that we have a virtue but will have to step out of our comfort zone of inertia to actively practice both goodness and good works that exemplify the virtues we want. This is a lifelong struggle that never ends.

There are many recognized Christian virtues such as

prudence, justice, temperance, courage, faith, hope, and charity (benevolence, generosity or sacrifice), chastity or purity (abstinence), diligence or persistence, patience, forgiveness, kindness (mercy and compassion), and humility or modesty. You can target many virtues for cultivation. For instance, you can try to cultivate gentleness by giving up the need to be right once you believe that being kind is more important than being correct and winning a confrontation. Mindfulness can help you do this. In Galatians you can find another list of virtues so these are just representative of those you can cultivate in yourself through this technique. Cultivating virtues is the same as cultivating inner beauty and nobility of character.

Padre Pio said, "The person who meditates and turns his mind to God, who is the mirror of his soul, seeks to know his faults, tries to correct them, moderates his impulses, and puts his conscience in order." This is the objective of this daily effort. One first starts with self-correction of their own faults, and then further works at developing virtuous characteristics that they lack. This is how one learns to live by love and tread the Christian path, which differs from all others in part because it centers around good works and self-perfection.

Typically monks and nuns simply work at eliminating their faults in a quiet protected enclosure, cloistered at distance from the world, so that without the distractions of society they can fully engage in the inner work of slowly transforming away their imperfections. This is not a process of quick success. Like irregularities on precious stones, our rough parts must first be hewn off before the final product can be gradually polished to shine. The problem is that we are not just inundated with imperfections, but constantly assaulted by worldly desires and passions that tempt us and distract us from progress. A monastic community, however, provides a protected environment within which we can work on ourselves.

The actual process of achieving spiritual maturity or perfection, whereby you eventually become so purified that you feel a constant energy of spiritual renewal in your body and mind, marks the very initial stages of spiritual progress that lead to *theosis*. These efforts can bring about that necessary vital stirring, so do not be alarmed if your efforts invite a response from Heaven.

Meditation also has the attainment of mental purity and the arrival of the Holy Spirit as its objectives, as does the activity of reverence during worship when we are to sacrificially give over our very being to God in adoration. When we worship God we should give ourselves over to the Father and hold nothing back as our egoistic own, but instead sacrifice our self-importance by emptying ourselves of all thoughts, concerns and will. During that sacrifice of the small self, like Jesus we will then fill with the Holy Spirit and God's presence.

Using this particular system of self-cultivation will polish our ethical and moral life, and our way of being in the world. By attention to self-correction, together with the power of God's sanctifying grace, a virtuous man or woman will pass through various spiritual stages and eventually cleanse themselves of the corrupting influences in their life. They will prepare themselves for *theosis* by a cathartic purification of their mind and behavior.

This method helps us subdue anger and hate, extinguish lust, and transform our carnal nature of passions and desires. It helps us cleanse our desires, move away from toxic tendencies, and transcend our normal self-centeredness so that it is replaced by a natural helpfulness and love for others. It helps us achieve a constant transformation of our lives into the life of Christ.

This practice will move us toward the good, for it will not only purify us but strengthen our virtuous nature. With a will of devoted commitment, and with the blessing of the holy powers, we can through this method of mindful self-correction move towards more perfect goodness. The continuous endeavor at repentance and reform of your faults, failings, and bad habits will, through God's matchless grace and the intercession of the saints, in time help you achieve the transformations required for *theosis*.

CONTINUOUS PRACTICE

This effort of self-watchfulness and self-adjustment must be carried out continuously. Like the need to eradicate robbers and thieves, you must resolve to wipe out your faults completely. During idle moments, and certainly during a time of daily review, you must search out and discover each and every selfish thought that feeds your pride, your desire for recognition, your desire for control, your selfish impulses and the like. You must become aware of your own thinking processes and assess them for propriety. You must discover the reasons behind your various actions that go against your wisdom and higher nature - such as mistaken beliefs, attitudes and prejudices or bad habits - and then work to dissolve those tendencies and replace them with something better.

Your conscience bears witness to your motivations and justifications throughout the day, so you must always keep a close eye on not just policing what you are doing but your intentions as well. You must resolve to pluck out and cast away the root of any sicknesses discovered and thereby dissolve the source of your improper habits through both the wisdom of analysis and remorse so that they can never arise again. A deep spiritual comfort and mental clarity will grow within you as long as you continue with this disciplined effort.

Employing this practice one must be, at all times, like a cat catching mice who has eyes intently watching and ears intently listening. As soon as a single improper thought begins to stir, you must conquer it and cast it out. Cut it off, transform it, change your attention, occupy yourself with something else such as prayer … there are many ways to deal with the pollutions that arise with us. Often you can catch yourself going astray and cut off inclinations at that moment, but in most cases it will take many instances to learn how to cut off the strong momentum of errant tendencies. You want to truly transform your habit energies and recurrent afflictions at their root.

There are many ways to transform old habits and become new, but it is a struggle. The stories of the saints show that their efforts to live just the commandments alone were not easy, and here we ask of much more. Many of their stories recount a fierce struggle to overcome negative tendencies such as anger, pride, selfishness, judgment of others and the pull of the passions. They recount how difficult it is to extend your love, kindness, care and compassion beyond yourself to others, but the Christian way is that the love you normally find in your family is to be extended to all others including strangers. The stirring of empathy within you must, through the road of Christian perfection, be turned into the benevolent love exemplified by the Good Samaritan. All your relationships must be characterized by consideration, compassion and care and it is through your involvement with the greater community of mankind that you can test such spiritual characteristics.

It is difficult to become interested in morality, justice, compassion, and other people's welfare rather than your own self-interests, and to become someone who is considered exemplary in personal conduct. Difficult it may seem, nevertheless this is our spiritual goal. Holiness is attainable after a definite struggle to attain self-mastery over your thoughts, emotions and behavior. It means returning to a condition of propriety, purity and rectitude. You must learn to always look within yourself, evaluate your own thinking and behavior and correct what errors you find. A person starts to become more refined when they start correcting their errant tendencies and devote themselves to this pursuit of consummate conduct.

The point is not to indulge in or accommodate improper thoughts or emotions in any way when they arise within your mind. They arise automatically so are not your fault. However, do not harbor them because harboring is the fault. Do not allow them a place in yourself they might call home. Do not create new errant habit energies either but work to correct your old ones. Recognize your faults, strive to eliminate them, and through this effort become humble to your fallibility while committed to change. Your job is to untie your knots of unwholesome behavior, and especially your ego attachments, because that is where your habit energies are centered. Doing so, it will become easier to cultivate moral qualities and propriety.

It is hard to break your ingrained thinking patterns, typical emotional responses, and habitual behaviors, but you can use this method to identify them and then with wisdom can work to replace them. You don't want to have to constantly suppress bad thinking or behavioral patterns, but want to transform the roots of errant behaviors so that they don't arise in the future. You want to eliminate those impulses entirely or replace them with something better.

It is said that a great man realizes when he makes a mistake, admits it, and having admitted it then corrects it. This is essentially the very same process of *catharsis* or purgation of which we are speaking, and it depends upon a daily "examination of conscience." The entire method is a process of awareness, remorse, contrition and correction. The objective is to pursue an advanced level of self-mastery, and to achieve it. You are to learn how to honestly evaluate your own behavior, how to stop taking your perspective as the right one in all situations, and how to think before acting. You are to learn how to reflect upon and work on your life.

Your thoughts, words and actions will become the house you live in, and here you are asked to renovate your house so that it becomes much more beautiful. There is a famous saying, "Beware thoughts, for they become words. Beware words, for they become our actions. Beware actions, for they become our habits. Beware habits, for they become our character." Also, "You sow an action and reap a tendency. You sow a tendency and reap a habit. You sow a habit and reap your character." This is what you are working to rectify. This whole process of self-observation and self-correction is about attaining self-mastery. You want to learn how to master the proper expression of your energies.

Those who undertake the daily practice of self-observation and self-rectification will by degrees understand themselves in a better way, learn from their mistakes, become able to avoid negative thinking, and develop the ability to control their thoughts, emotions and behavior. By growing in this way, they will also experience more happiness and well-being in their lives.

Through this technique of watchful attention and self-correction, as well as the opening of yourself to God through meditation and prayer, one truly begins to live a holy life and becomes truly holy. It is through a continual self-effort that this purification comes about.

You *must become committed* to mindfulness and self-correction, making them a central part of your spiritual efforts. You must discipline yourself with a daily review of your behavior where you spot your faults and correct them. From these efforts, in time your mind and behavior will subsequently become purified. Your relationships with others will improve as well. In all your efforts, remember that helping a brother monk or sister nun who is ill or struggling takes priority over your own personal concerns and considerations. This is the purpose of the spiritual life, which is that the problems of others should become our own problems.

St. Bernard had taught: "As a searching investigator of the integrity of your own conduct, submit your life to a daily examination. Consider carefully what progress you have made or what ground you have lost. Strive to know yourself. Place all your faults before your eyes. Come face to face with yourself, as though you were another person, and then weep for your faults." Weeping for your faults means acknowledging your personal errors, feeling shame and contrition, vowing to change and then doing so. This will help satisfy our thirst for the attainment of virtue and the peace of conscience. We must all submit ourselves continuously to the spiritual practice of self-correction.

Through a heightened spiritual awareness of God, being constantly aware that He is always with us and knows all that we do, and being in constant remembrance of Him in your thoughts and deeds, you will have the power to succeed in this practice. When what is before you seems difficult because of your ego then give up your ego by emptying yourself so that God becomes the higher doer. The more energy put into satisfying your ego the less energy there is available to advance in one's spiritual transformation. Empty yourself of yourself when the path is difficult and submit your will to God's will when it is difficult to break your patterns, for He wants you to achieve incorruption.

This activity of spiritual training is a type of reverence for God by pursuing a faultlessness that will give form to righteous living. In our efforts to improve ourselves we should remember our inherent union with God's faultlessness which makes purity possible. You therefore must ask, at the time of daily review and confession, to be blessed by God's grace so that your will can become His own and you can succeed with this continuous effort. It will become easier as time goes on.

This practice of continually being mindful or observant of your inner and outer behavior for the purposes of self-correction makes you more pleasing in the eyes of God. To submit oneself to correction is not only a humbling type of purification towards self-improvement, but a form of devotional submission to God preparing you for *theoria* and *theosis*. In committing to the "Way of Perfection," this practice is your foundation.

The spiritual goal for the human nature is that you become ennobled, majestic, Christ-like. The goal is that you become an exemplary individual with princely qualities because you always exhibit a joy of life and irreproachable, consummate conduct – the very best behavior you can express – permeated by kindness, concern, care and compassion for others. As an individual following a spiritual calling you have an extra degree of responsibility in how you should behave because your demeanor and conduct serve as models for the community. Remember that we are to serve as lighthouses for the world.

This method of spiritual self-correction amounts to a divinization of our behavior, which necessary within the process to *theosis*. It enables us to practice and actually live the teachings of Christ rather than just remain at an inert stage of stale theoretical knowledge.

Every day you must engage in a remembrance of any wrongs and slights you may have committed such as instances of anger, ego, slander, greed, laziness, pride, and so forth. You must also start becoming conscious of what you are doing every moment, spotting your inherent weaknesses in present time, and understanding your motivations or reasons why you do the things you do or act in the way you act. Christianity asks us to work at self-improvement when we discover faults in ourselves by summoning the strength and spirit to overcome them. This we must do in real time.

St. Ignatius of Loyola, in his *Spiritual Exercises*, laid out a similar technique of introspective repentance that also involves the steps of self-observation, self-correction, self-examination, contrition and then the hard work of self-development or self-improvement. According to his teachings, followers must first thank God for the benefits He has bestowed upon them such as the gift of consciousness itself; second, they must ask for the grace of clear awareness to be able to know and correct their faults and errant tendencies; third, they must at the end of the day pass in mental review the successive hours of the day, noting what faults they have committed in deed, word, thought, or omission; fourth, they must ask God's pardon for their wrong responses; fifth, they must purpose amendment.

Purgation is the gradual submission of a person to the good, and *theosis* is the final result. Purgation is a reforming of one's character, a process of self-correction that is part of the process of self-mastery and self-improvement. Spiritual aspirants who work hard at abandoning their ego through meditation and submit to the *catharsis* of self-correction eventually attain deification after passing through stages of purification and illumination. Purification makes it possible to invite in divine grace, which one starts experiencing in *theoria*, because of pursuing a purity in conduct like this that strengthens your relationship with God.

Peter said, "Repent and be baptized, every one of you, in the name of Jesus Christ for the forgiveness of your sins. And you will receive the gift of the Holy Spirit. The promise is for you and your children and for all who are far off-for all whom the Lord our God will call" (Acts 2). Through self-correction we will invite upon ourselves the visitation of the Holy Spirit.

CHAPTER 6

MENTAL AND CONTEMPLATIVE PRAYER FOR ATTAINING *THEORIA*

Saint Seraphim of Sarov once said, "However prayer, fasting, vigil and all the other Christian practices may be, they do not constitute the aim of our Christian life. Although it is true that they serve as the indispensible means of reaching this end, the true aim of our Christian life consists of the acquisition of the Holy Spirit of God. As for fasts, and vigils, and prayer, and almsgiving, and every good deed done for Christ's sake, are the only means of acquiring the Holy Spirit of God. ... Of course, every good deed done for Christ's sake gives us the grace of the Holy Spirit, but prayer gives us this grace most of all, for it is always at hand, as an instrument for acquiring the grace of the Spirit. ... we must pray only until God the Holy Spirit descends on us in measures of His heavenly grace known to Him."

The essential purpose of prayer is to place yourself in

God's presence and to remain there, raising your mind and heart solely to God. During prayer you can ask for his help in various matters, or ask for His transformative powers and await His influence through the Holy Spirit. Just as we cannot sit before a fire without becoming warm, the spirit of His presence is active and vivifying, and prayer brings us into that holy presence. It will heal and sanctify you. The monastic tradition has the purpose of leading you to seamless union with His presence every moment of the day, and this becomes possible after being consistently trained in such a way that your ego and self-centered thoughts no longer stand in the way.

Luke 5:16 says that "Jesus often withdrew to lonely places and prayed." From His example we can know that prayer is not just for priests, monks and nuns, but is for everyone including children. Unfortunately, few know how to pray correctly and need some simple directions.

The Christian tradition espouses three major types of prayer: vocal prayer, mental prayer, and contemplative prayer that we should correctly call meditation or centering prayer. The reasons for this change in terminology is that thinking is contemplation whereas being free of thought is properly called meditation practice, which is practicing an internal quietude of the mind rather than engaging in active thinking.

All types of pondering, rumination and intellectual analysis are properly classified as contemplation. Therefore although the standard Christian vocabulary divides mental prayer into meditation (active mental prayer) and contemplation (passive mental prayer), the terms should be reversed and are done so in this book.

Francis of Sales said: "Begin all prayer, whether mental

or vocal, by an act of the Presence of God. If you observe this rule strictly, you will soon see how useful it is." Ignatius of Loyola also began each of his Spiritual Exercises with a "Preparatory Prayer" that requires you to first place yourself in the presence of God. This is excellent practice and recommended.

Furthermore, all Christian prayer methods should be followed by a silent time of internal sacred quietude, which can be transformative. By means of this stillness your mind will touch calmness, and your ability to see the reality of situations and make more accurate judgments will be enhanced in that peaceful clarity. Practicing the humility of internal silence, where you abandon thoughts to rest in the peace of God's presence, cannot just lead to spiritual intuitions but is the forerunner of *theoria*.

It is essential to understand that prayer can have different purposes, which is why there are different types of prayer, but most all forms of transformative prayer should eventually lead to an abandonment of thoughts and an experience of mental quiet that is *theoria*, a type of internal illumination where you are mentally quiet but filled with tremendous peace and clarity due to achieving some degree of unity with God. It is in that silence that God pours himself into us, and by humbly putting ourselves aside we experience communion with God from that poverty of ego assertions. This is the ultimate purpose of the highest form of prayer – union with God.

The four basic forms of prayer are that of blessing and adoration (praise), petition (supplication), intercession, and thanksgiving. Prayer may be expressed either vocally or mentally so it is also divided into two types, vocal and mental. Vocal prayer may be spoken or sung, such as when chanting hymns. Mental prayer can take the form of either silent meditation or thoughtful contemplation.

Vocal prayer comes from the mouth, and normally involves the repetition of an established set of words and phrases that are either read or recited from memory. Examples of vocal prayers are when you verbally recite the Lord's Prayer (Our Father, Pater Noster), Hail Mary (Ave Maria), Glory Be (Gloria Patri), Apostles' Creed rosary, or the Prayer of the Heart. As you recite, the continual repetitions of the spoken prayer can calm your mind by quieting your thoughts, and can produce a harmonizing influence on the energy and sensations felt within you. To have this happen you must abandon the practice of letting your thoughts wander by intently focusing on the meaning of the prayers when reciting them.

MENTAL PRAYER

Mental prayer takes place wholly within your mind. It is an internal form of spiritual practice where you repeatedly recite words only within your mind. It is said that all the saints have become saints by mental prayer, and that without the aid of mental prayer the soul cannot triumph over sensual indulgences, carnal desires and the forces of corruption. Saint John of the Cross said, "Without the aid of mental prayer, the soul cannot triumph over the forces of the demon."

Saint Alphonsus Liguori said, "All the Saints have become Saints by mental prayer," and further commented, "It is morally impossible for him who neglects meditation to live without sin." He added that, because it is incompatible with sin no one can continue the practice of mental prayer and continue committing wrongs. They will either repent of their faults or quit the practice of mental prayer. Therefore, both prayer and meditation go together as partners with the reflective practice of self-correction, and these practices must become an essential part of your daily spiritual exercises.

The function of mental prayer is to transform your personality, thoughts and attitudes and thereby effect a profound change in your heart and dispositions. This pursuit is a lifelong process. Saint Peter of Alcantara said, "In mental prayer, the soul is purified from its sins, nourished with charity, confirmed in faith, and strengthened in hope; the mind expands, the affections dilate, the heart is purified, truth becomes evident; temptation is conquered, sadness dispelled; the senses are renovated; drooping powers revive; tepidity ceases; the rust of vices disappears. Out of mental prayer issues forth, like living sparks, those desires of heaven which the soul conceives when inflamed with the fire of divine love. Sublime is the excellence of mental prayer, great are its privileges; to mental prayer heaven is opened; to mental prayer heavenly secrets are manifested and the ear of God [is] ever attentive."

St. John Climacus said that prayer is a familiar conversation with God wherein the soul converses with God, and God with the soul. Therefore, rather than always reciting a standard prayer formula, sometimes prayers should express your own sentiments in the form of a private conversation between you and God, a type of internal conversational dialogue. Teresa of Avila's said, "prayer is nothing else than a close sharing between friends; it means taking time frequently to be alone with him who we know loves us," and so it is proper to talk to God during prayer and fully express yourself in that conversation.

In mental prayer we can speak freely with God, sometimes in supplication, and in return He may offer assistance by shedding light upon our troubles, or envelop us with a profound peace as His way of comforting us. It is in that silence that God pours himself into us, which is ultimately the purpose of most forms of repetitive prayer.

Allowing God to be fully present within you is at the core of the highest levels of prayer because in prayer the true protagonist is God. "What matters in prayer is not what we do but what God does in us during those moments," said Jacques Philippe in *Time for God*. Placing oneself in God's presence and remaining there is the essential act of prayer for that is when He transforms us. In vocal prayer we speak to God, but in mental prayer He speaks to us because we silence ourselves and let God pour Himself into us to dominate the conversation.

Mental prayer can either be a direct speaking to God, or a form of meditative quiet where we cultivate a deeper connection to God through inner silence. Sometimes this silence is called contemplative prayer or centering prayer. In this form of prayer you abandon yourself to a total poverty of self-dialogue, giving away all of your thoughts and holding onto nothing just as you might give away everything you have to charity.

This is one of the meanings of the monastic vows of poverty. Because of this emptying of your mind where you are giving away the thought-stream products of your ego, "putting off your own will," God will immediately become most fully present as a substitute to fill in the void. This is how you develop your relationship with God and work to reach *theoria*.

This type of "imageless" or "thought-free" mental prayer involves centering ourselves in pure faith without any preconceived notions of God or other expectations. We just give up everything that arises within the mind and wait without expectations, refusing to attach to anything. This is the true spiritual poverty loved by the Lord.

Elder Aimilianos of Simonopetra said, "The meaning of 'pure prayer' has the same sense that is given to it by all the (Christian Church) Fathers. Pure prayer means prayer that is free of thoughts, prayer that does not introduce any outside elements; it contains no mental forms, shapes or images. Pure prayer is not the personal property of monks or a small group of individuals. It is for everyone; it is the one activity that is the most fitting to the human person."

When we give up all thoughts and enter into the natural silence of our mind, all our internal dialogue gradually fades away into a spiritual tranquility. That abandonment of thoughts by giving all our concerns over to God should be considered a sacrificial act of offering and surrender. This type of practice will help us reach a state of supreme solitude centered entirely on the presence of God, which is how we can reach the experience of God in *theoria*. Thus, Saint Paisios the Anthonite regularly said to younger monks, "You know, the whole essence, the secret of monastic life is in obedience, cutting off your will. Then the grace of God comes."

CONTEMPLATIVE PRAYER

Another type of prayer is contemplative prayer or

contemplation, which is more active in reflections because you mentally analyze and ponder over some topic. Contemplation applies our imaginative capabilities, our memory and our understanding to consider some spiritual principle, question or problem. It can also be used to help decide an issue and resolve on some course of action. Or, during a period of contemplation you can hold a steady thought in your mind like an immeasurable emotion, or a visualized image such as the Passion of Christ, in order to envelop yourself within a particular state of concentration. When you practice this form of prayer you need to hold onto that one large thought-emotion with stability and let it permeate even the energy of your body while eschewing all other distractions.

As with meditative prayer, the ultimate form of contemplative prayer is an internal silence, without thoughts, centered entirely on the presence of God. Thus, contemplative practice also has a purgative aspect to because its highest form requires us to free ourselves from wandering thoughts and ultimately empty our minds. Typically you are to concentrate upon some thought or image during contemplative prayer, but the highest form of contemplation is to remain totally centered in God who cannot be fathomed by remaining within a peaceful mental silence.

Prayer can lead you into experiencing many types of spiritual states. This includes moments of profound stillness, raptures or ecstasies, and even a type of cessation of the senses where all of existence disappears from your mind. During prayer you might smell wondrous fragrant odors, hear heavenly singing, see visions of the saints and angelic beings, feel heat and cold within your body, taste your saliva becoming sweet within your mouth, and more. When these occur you should pay no importance to such phenomena because God, the target and purpose of *theosis*, is beyond the five senses.

Basically, the function of prayer is to transform your heart to make *theoria* possible, and then *theosis*. This is the purpose of the holy life, and is a lifelong process to achieve this.

Remember that there are many possible uses for prayer, but the *theosis* of unity with God is the ultimate target of all spiritual practices. *Theoria* is attained prior to *theosis*, and is achieved due to the cultivation of meditation, mindful watchfulness over your thinking and conduct, chanting, prayer and other spiritual practices that together prepare you to start experiencing the sacred quietude of spiritual union with God. Once you achieve that union, the blessed energies of the Holy Spirit will arrive and start transforming your body and soul in miraculous ways. Chanting and internal exercises of ablution should also become part of your preparatory efforts for *catharsis*, *theoria* and *theosis*.

St. Ignatius of Loyola in his *Spiritual Exercises* has as a basic principle that "the Lord communicates himself to the well-disposed person," but you only become "well-disposed" if you engage in a variety of spiritual exercises that lead to inner purification. An aspirant should strive to transform their character, their thinking and their behavior to become more pleasing in the eyes of God. They should be working at purifying the deeper elements of their nature.

Remember what Saint Seraphim said – "As for fasts, and vigils, and prayer, and almsgiving, and every good deed done for Christ's sake, are the only means of acquiring the Holy Spirit of God." The ultimate purpose of all spiritual work both inside and outside of the monastic or celebratory environment is firstly *theoria*. In the *theoria* of communion you will experience God directly including the "uncreated light" of His Spirit. What will also arrive are the energies of the Holy Spirit. The transformations due to the energies of the Holy Spirit are part of the necessary process of *catharsis* and *theoria* that then lead to *theosis*.

PRAYER PRACTICE

Some types of prayer involve constantly repeating a single word such as "Christos," or reciting a phrase with a feeling so deep that it penetrates your mind and soul. For instance, you can do this using Scriptural verses such as "God is love" (1 John 4:16). Instead of a scriptural phrase or passage, the author of *The Cloud of Unknowing* recommended use of a monosyllabic word, such as just "God" or "Love." When reciting a word, phrase, scriptural passage or complete prayer you should always listen to it intently and focus your mind on the meaning of the prayer inside you.

Saint John Cassian recommended reciting the prayer, "O God, make speed to save me: O Lord, make haste to help me" ("O God, come to my assistance; O Lord, make haste to help me"). The Greek Orthodox Church recommends, "Most Holy Theotokis (Mary), help us." The Portuguese have a common prayer, "O deus ego amo te" – "O God I love thee." Different traditions have different prayer preferences.

An extremely popular and powerful recommendation is the Jesus Prayer: "Lord Jesus Christ, Son of God, have mercy on me." There is no standardization for the exact words of this prayer but the words used should invoke an attitude of modesty and humility that is essential for the attainment of *theoria*.

This is a very powerful prayer with many variants, and has been used by countless Church Fathers and saints. The basic recitation technique is to put your mind into your heart and rhythmically recite the prayer in tune with your breathing, "Lord Jesus Christ, Son of God, have mercy on me."

The Jesus Prayer will help invoke within you an attitude of humility where you abandon your ego and self-will. When recited continuously, it can lead to an unceasing prayer within your heart where the recitation automatically continues on its own without any effort on your part. In other words, after you continuously recite the prayer it can then become an automatic Unceasing Prayer within you, which is an attainment that Paul the Apostle advocates in the New Testament.

It is usually an experienced Church Elder who will teach you how recite the Jesus Prayer with your *nous* to experience the unceasing Prayer of the Heart. They will teach you how to invite the grace of God into yourself by reciting the prayer, and what that experience will be like. The normal instructions are that you must constantly recite the prayer for up to seven or eight hours daily while keeping your *nous*, or mind, centered in either your heart or upon the meaning of the prayer, and it must be recited in synchrony with your breathing.

As stated, after you recite the prayer long enough with

spiritual feeling and concentration, it may spontaneously become "self-active." You might hear it automatically recited within your head, chest or heart, which is one of the reasons it is called the Prayer of the Heart. It will start operating continuously inside you on its own and energy may also start rising spontaneously within you. This is a sure sign of progress towards deification that marks a definite visitation of the Holy Spirit.

In other words, through constant recitation you will attain what the Apostle Paul called "unceasing prayer," which is accompanied by the continual movement of the Holy Spirit within you washing your body like currents of energy. You might also taste a sweetness in your mouth due to a committed recitation or from other spiritual practices, or you might experience heavenly visions such as the Sacred Heart of Jesus inside you.

Following Christ's instruction to "go into your room, close the door and pray to your Father, who is unseen. Then your Father, who sees what is done in secret, will reward you" (Matthew 6:6), those who want to practice the Prayer of the Heart should often withdraw into solitude for recitation, which also means an aloneness without thoughts. By means of a solitude of inner quiet, your mind will become calmed and come closer to God.

Hesychast practice, which is also known as noetic prayer, is a name given to this powerful spiritual practice of reciting the Jesus Prayer while simultaneously emptying your mind completely. With this prayer method you can also intensely focus on the meaning of the prayer as you recite it, or simply listen to the words while emptying your mind of other thoughts. There are different traditions as to how you should practice the Jesus Prayer, and spiritual elders often vary slightly as to the instructions they will teach others.

Similar to a meditation practice, according to one technique a practitioner should recite the Jesus Prayer in silence and with eyes closed while being "empty of mental pictures" and concepts. Another way to recite the prayer is by intensely focusing on the meaning of the words during each and every recitation. Another method is to free the mind of thoughts and recite the words while simply listening to the sounds, which will eventually make your thoughts die down so that your mind becomes quiet and peaceful.

While practicing the Jesus Prayer, a Hesychast should cultivates *nepsis*, which is a watchful attention of your mind that rejects tempting thoughts that might pull you away from concentrating on the prayer. *Nepsis* is basically a type of mindfulness or concentration practice of sustained focus and attention. While reciting, a Hesychast must focus only upon the prayer and pay attention to the contents of their mind. They must stay focused on the prayer and not let their mind wander in any way. They must remain undistracted by things outside themselves and not give in to disturbances, annoyances or agitations that might normally affect them, which is how one advances spiritually. A monastic life entails working to overcome mental distractions since they can disturb the mind of purity that we want to cultivate.

Since earliest times, each Christian monastic tradition has recommended a different amount of prayer time per day. Some monastic traditions have made prayer the center of their community life while others have considered it only an auxiliary practice. In some Christian monasteries, men and women gather three to seven times daily to pray the psalms, but in some traditions the monastics pray for only half an hour during the morning and evening. Teresa of Avila recommended praying for two hours daily, so you can see that traditions differ on the amount of time to be spent at prayer.

The purest prayer is that which is free of thoughts, which does not introduce any outside elements of mental forms, shapes or images. This is the type of prayer suitable for everyone, but it takes work to develop this ability. This type of prayer practice is how you become closest to God.

When you disentangle your self from your thoughts and material things, and stand before God in this way, you will experience a greater share of His peace and divine energies, which are God's response to your efforts. After much repeated practice, the response of energy flowing inside you will feel like "the spring of water that wells up to eternal life."

The aim of every prayer is this acquisition of the Holy Spirit. When the Holy Spirit starts operating within an individual and commences upon the true holy process of purgation, even their bones will become sanctified while their physical body will attain incorruptibility. This is the pathway to beatitude and glorification. This is how God cleanses us and produces saints.

Remember the words of Saint Seraphim of Sarov once again, "If prayer and watching gives you more grace of God's grace, watch and pray; if fasting gives you much of the spirit God, fast; if almsgiving gives you more, give alms. Weigh every virtue done for Christ's sake in this manner."

CHAPTER 7

PRAYERFUL CHANTING SHOULD DEEPLY MOVE YOUR ENERGY AND EMOTIONS

In the book *Human Sounds*, Jonathan Goldman recounted how a group of French Benedictine monks abandoned their daily six hours of traditional chanting in order to free up their time for more useful, productive activities. Afterwards, they quickly became fatigued and depressed. Once they resumed their chanting, on the advice of a doctor, they quickly regained their prior energy and positivity.

The reason the Benedictine monks had become depressed is because chanting lifts your mood and moves your internal energy, which is an essential part of the process towards *theoria* and then *theosis*. Once the chanting ceases and you then stop moving the energy inside you, you will feel the loss tangibly and experience a sense of despondency.

Because chanting moves both your emotions and energy, chanting is not just rewarding but formative for the holy life. It balances your emotions, leads to internal quiet, and helps to keep you healthy. Once you get used to the melodic sounds of chanting that on a daily basis break up internal stagnation and move your energy around inside your body, its absence is as if you lost a part of your being.

While chanting as a form of worship certainly unites the monastic community, from the French Benedictine experience we can clearly understand that one of the other powerful purposes of chanting – although little discussed – is this ability to move your emotions *and* your internal energy. This will produce a wonderful *catharsis* of your inner being that in an inexplicable way prepares you for *theoria*. Knowing this, now you need to learn how to chant in a way that maximizes this potential, such as chanting's ability to arouse sacred feelings and move your internal body energy so that this form of worship will bring greater blessings to you.

Saint Benedict mentions that in chanting your mind has to be in tune with your voice, which requires practice. In particular, you must pay attention to how you are singing every moment. Whether your voice is good or bad doesn't make any difference – what is important is if your mind and my heart are disconnected, whether the chanting is moving your energy and mood, and whether it is harmonizing your energy and spirit.

Chanting has two possible afterwards: it should lead you to either prayer or prepare you for meditative silence. To accomplish either of these purposes, your mind has to be in tune with both your voice and energy when chanting, and it takes practice to achieve this harmonization with the melodies. It takes practice to learn the proper intonations and pitches that will stir your vital energies and harmonize your spirit, so chanting is a discipline in the sense that you have to work at to get good at it just like most things in life. Thus, chanting is a form of self-development work in addition to a form of worship. It is a purification technique because it can calm or uplift your emotions and fill you with a positive energy that will wash your soul with goodness. Few monks or nuns will tell you these facts, just as few can tell you the secrets to practicing noetic prayer (the unceasing Prayer of the Heart).

During chanting you must practice the tonal singing correctly while also feeling the sound energy penetrate everywhere inside you to touch or "wash" all the parts of your body with that energy. Specifically, you must sing so that the sound power touches different areas of your body during the melodic intonations. At the same time, you have to put your soul into it and welcome deep emotions that raise you toward the spiritual world. Mark 12:30 instructs us, "Love the Lord your God with all your heart, all your soul, all your mind and with all your strength," so you must charge all your thoughts, sensations and emotions with the power of the melody in order to transcend your worldly mentality. Since most chanting sounds are naturally felt primarily in the upper part of your body, you must work hard over time to spread the penetration of sound energy down into your arms and hands, lower abdomen, and even your legs and feet.

Most people never extend their vocal energy down into their lower abdomen and pelvis, but over time you must work to make the vibrations felt within these areas. Over time you can learn to originate the sound power from within all body regions. In fact, while chanting you should eventually feel the harmonious melodies vibrating within every cell of your body while you are simultaneously permeated with a strong feeling of joy, delight, triumph, harmony, reverence, sadness, animation, awe, solemnity, holiness, peacefulness or whatever other positive or negative modes naturally arise in response. When you chant, do it with full emotions and feelings.

These feelings matter. You must try to fully feel the emotions evoked during chanting even if you are repeating the same chants day after day for year after year and might feel a bit bored from the repetition. Eventually chanting will break open your heart so that your energy and emotions flow more freely inside you. The emotions evoked through chanting will help you move your internal energy, and daily repetition of chanting will give you a chance to get good at this so that you can use the energy to "wash" all the areas of your body.

Three songs everyone knows serve as examples of how sounds should cascade within your body. When singing "O Come, O Come Emmanuel," Shubert's "Ave Maria," or the "Gloria, in Excelsis Deo" refrain from "Angels We Have Heard on High," the sounds are projected from different parts of your body. We feel wonderful from projecting sounds from different parts of our body, and by the end of the chanting the energies within our disparate body parts should be meshed together as one unified spirit. When performing chants we should try to move the sounds inside us to wash all the parts of our interior with both sound energies *and* deep emotions. We should also try, when chanting, to feel the entire energy of our body as one whole. It takes years of practice to get to this stage, but every time you chant you should make progress towards this full-bodied feeling of resonating energy and deep emotions within you.

You must perform chanting with heightened attention of the intent to move your internal energy, or the sound power, everywhere within your body in intimate union with the melody. You should try to feel the sound power affecting everywhere inside you including within your hands and feet, where Jesus was nailed on the cross. In this way you can use the power of the melodies to not only evoke powerful feelings but to fully stimulate your complete body in a very harmonious way.

Sometimes you should totally forget yourself so that the sounds fully penetrate you without being constrained by your thoughts and thinking. This will prepare you for quiet meditation afterwards. This takes practice and is one of the untaught principles of chanting that makes it an essential portion of *purgatio* in holy preparation for *theoria*, an illuminative union with God.

With chanting, everything should contribute to producing a gentle rhythm and harmonious flow that will help you enter into prayer afterwards, or prepare you for entering into silence. The rhythmic breathing that chanting requires, and its tonal modalities that smoothen your body's energies, can transport you to a peaceful stillness that is a perfect setup for meditation practice. The daily ritual of chanting will harmonize your internal energy, and after achieving that feeling of fullness together with silence you can prepare for the union of *theoria*, but only if your mind, emotions and energy all become balanced. Chanting is perfectly designed to produce an internal silence that can transform into a profound communion with God.

Sounds do not become music until they enter a person and move their mind. In other words, music exists only because your mind interacts with sounds and interprets them in a special way. Chanting evokes meaningful responses in your thoughts and feelings because you have a mind, so you must use your mind to help the sounds become the most useful they can possibly be. They can move the light inside you and take you into your deepest interior. You must learn how to move the sound energy everywhere inside you by chanting with emotion while projecting the sounds from larger and larger areas inside your body that should be vibrated by the words sung.

Basically, monks and nuns can experience profound reverence through chanting or song, and can use this reverence along with the sound power to internally cleanse themselves, which is another type of purgation leading to *theosis*. The way you sing and what you sing, or what you chant and how you chant, are essential in helping you accomplish this.

Because it helps to harmonize your energy and mood, chanting produces inner calmness and tranquility. It can fill your mind with quiet spiritual moods that will free your thinking for higher spiritual states of union with God, *theoria*. In other words, by daily absorbing yourself in the simple undulating melodies and using them to harmonize your interior states, over time the mental quiet it produces will deepen and lead to *theoria*. Your mind will become less and less filled with wandering thoughts, and thus deepen in quietude to prepare you for the *theoria* of illumination.

Chanting takes many forms in the Christian spiritual tradition. There are Gregorian, Byzantine, Anglican, Znamenny and many other types of chants. In fact, most religions, regardless of their differences in dogmas and beliefs, have various forms of spiritual singing and chanting because they are a way of coming closer to God. Most religions through prayer and song request God's presence and blessing at mealtimes, at weddings, and in other ceremonial or holy moments. Each group is hoping for a profound and unifying experience.

The key commonality in these various forms of spiritual singing, which includes Gospel music, is that they move both your emotions *and* the energy within your body. That's the important thing. When you start singing or chanting you can be transported to an entirely new emotional realm, a brand new state of mind. Chanting can be peaceful and calming, or strongly lift your spirits with great energy and enthusiasm, and you will often feel great energy inside you. You might also experience feelings of piety, solemnity, joyfulness, reverence, piety, majesty, gratitude, great delight and sometimes even negative emotions like sadness or grief.

People will often feel energy moving inside them when chanting, just as happens when you are visited by the Holy Spirit, and this energy might touch your body, mind and emotions in various ways we might call "holy" or "sacred." The positive moods and internal energy aroused through chanting can even sometimes heal illness. Every person is unique so their responses to chanting will be different.

These profound results do not usually occur with rock music, pop music, or with disharmonious melodies. It is only the spiritual music where the verses flow and rise, where the cadence brings you along and your breathing becomes rhythmical, where the prayers are flowing and your spirit becomes connected with God, that can comfort and heal you both emotionally and physically. In the gentle rhythms of Christian chanting, everything should come together and help you to enter into prayer, or prepare you for going into silence and tranquility.

Psalm 150 proclaims, "Let everything that has breath praise the Lord." The chanting of the psalms, hymns and so forth lauds the divine power, and intensifies the bonds within the community. No one can deny that chanting in the choir together as a group is a catalytic agent that achieves cohesion for a monastic community. It definitely unites everyone together. The homogenization of all voices into one voice is the very embodiment of the monastic ethos.

In order to chant together the brothers or sisters must listen to each other and respond with sincerity in pitch, volume, and nuance. Collectively, chanting threads together the community, reduces interpersonal conflicts and increases monastic camaraderie to create a more affirming, harmonious, and holistic environment. When the group achieves this, the brothers or sisters develop a sense of belonging that strengthens their bonds of unity. Saint Basil refers to the reconciling nature of community voices united by singing as contributing to a life of balance, spontaneous generosity, and benevolence. It is definitely a force for engendering brotherly love and cementing the mutual support of one another. Hence, there are many community benefits to chanting.

Attentive to the harmonious melodic singing, where the rhythmic breathing helps to move their internal states, a community involved in the act of chanting comes together as one and enters more easily in to the contemplative mind of prayer or meditation. This is a crucial purpose to chanting because the sounds of psalmody, readings, homilies, and hymns are always accentuated by periods of silence, and followed by a period of profound silence. These patterns of harmonious sound and then silence, where you can enter into God, should become the very routine or norm of the monastic space.

When your whole community is there praying together, chanting together and then silent together—this is the beauty of the monastic life.

Chanting together in a group is certainly a common monastic way of achieving group unity and feelings of well-being for all its members. It produces an internal effect for each individual as well as for the ritual environment, and since it influences your own progress towards *theoria*, this is the aspect you must emphasize for yourself. The rhythm of sounds and breathing required in chanting is a mechanism that can carry each person into his interior. Knowing this, you should chant in such a way that maximizes chanting's potential for doing this because inner silence is great spiritual progress

In the monastic and celebratory tradition, the internal purpose is the most important thing. That purpose in chanting includes transforming your emotions and internal energy to harmonize your mind and body. You want to use chanting to dissolve any feelings of internal blockage you feel inside your body, and to help you prepare for the true inner silence of *theoria*. This inner silence will surely influence everyone around you in a beneficial manner because they will feel it and then become peaceful themselves. Saint Seraphim of Sarov has told us, "Acquire a peaceful spirit and then thousands around you will be saved."

CHAPTER 8

INTERNAL SPIRITUAL EXERCISES

In Judaism, the initial part of the first of the Ten Commandments is, "Anokhi Yod Heh Vav Heh Elohekha" (lit. "I AM YHVH your God"). In the Jewish tradition, the forerunner of Christianity, men and women often recite a shortened version of this as a prayer spoken in rhythm with their breathing: "Ani Yod Heh Vav Heh." They recite the words rhythmically over and over again until their breathing and their thoughts both calm down.

In Christianity, the same practice of rhythmical praying is performed in countless holy houses using a variety of prayers, such as the popular Portuguese prayer, "O deus ego amo te" – "O God I love thee." For this prayer, the word "deus" might be replaced by "abba" to create "O abba ego amo te" instead.

Reciting this prayer continuously will help you to pacify your breathing and thoughts. However, there is an even more powerful step we can take for our spiritual progress.

As part of the road to *theosis*, we are all to become washed by the energies of the Holy Spirit, and therefore our external bodies of corruption are to be cleansed by God's healing energies in order to purify the indwelling soul. In the Bible, King Nebuchadnezzar had a dream where God showed that our physical bodies, born of the earth, were exceedingly corrupted. They are like a jumbled collection of disparate parts that don't join with each other as a single harmonious whole.

Daniel 2:31-33 says, "You, O King, were watching and beheld a giant statue. This great statue, whose splendor was dazzling, stood before you and its appearance was terrifying. This statue's head was of fine gold, its chest and arms of silver, its belly and his thighs of bronze, its legs of iron, its feet partly of iron and partly of clay."

The body in the king's dream reveals the state of man's corrupted, fallen nature due to the fact that our physical body is corrupted; it is not a unified spiritual whole. Instead it is composed of dissimilar humors whose energies are fractionated and disconnected from one another.

But just as chanting can unite the different members of our monastic communities, and listening to music can bring harmony to your mind and energy, we can use singing or chanting in a special way to dissolve the differences between the dissimilar parts of our bodies so that they finally feel energetically connected as a single whole. Because the life of a monk or nun revolves around communal ritual and hours of melodic chanting or songful prayer, given time they are sure to experience this.

We can and should use prayer recitations of "O abba ego amo te" to achieve this same result. In particular, based on the indications provided by this dream from the Lord, we can recite our prayers so that we feel the sounds in the same areas of our bodies that God has indicated in order to harmonize their dissimilar natures. In this way, by using sound energy to knead together our disparate parts that He has identified, we can start working to bring about a more harmonious unity to our being. We can use the power of sound to counter our internal degradation by harmonizing our whole body as one, just as the Holy Spirit must also wash our entire body with sacred energies to counter our corruptions.

Therefore in remembrance of the fact that we must all uplift ourselves from a state of degradation, you should recite the prayer "O abba ego amo te" as follows. The instructions involve reciting the sounds of the prayer in the specific sections of the body indicated by God and using our mental powers of focus and visualization at the same time.

When you recite the first word of the prayer, "O," do so feeling the sound within your head and simultaneously imagine that your entire head becomes the color of shining gold.

For the second word, "abba," recite it so as to feel its energies inside your chest and arms, which you should imagine to be shining like bright silver.

Next, recite and feel the sound of "ego" inside your belly and thighs, which you should imagine to shine with the color of yellowish bronze.

You should next recite and feel the vibration of "amo" in both your legs, imagined as black in color.

Lastly, you should recite and feel the sound of "te" inside your feet, which are imagined as being red in color.

Providing us with additional instruction, Daniel further recounts of the dream: "the feet that were of iron and clay were broken into pieces. Then was the iron, the clay, the brass, the silver, and the gold, broken to pieces together, and became like the chaff of the summer threshing floors; and the wind carried them away, that no place was found for them."

Since dust we are and unto dust we shall return, after performing many prayer repetitions in this fashion you should stop praying when you feel you have become full of energy, and then imagine that your body becomes dust that is blown away by the wind. Imagine that it scatters to leave nothing behind, and only empty space remains in the place of what was once your corrupted body. You should then remain within that state of empty quiescence, just as is done in the method of *Lectio Divina,* until the Holy Spirit moves you to return to normal.

JACOB'S LADDER

The Bible contains many instructions such as this whose meaning is only revealed to spiritual elders who have devoted their lives to cultivating the holy path, and who sometimes reveal such spiritual exercises to others. For instance, in another Biblical dream the Patriarch Jacob saw that a ladder was set upon the earth, and the top of it reached to the heavens. Upon the ladder he saw angels ascending and descending in and out of Heaven.

The spine of our body is that heavenly ladder that transmits nerve impulses up and down our body. It spans from our most earthly, carnal nature in the pelvis to our head that can create lofty thoughts of beauty and wisdom.

With our mind, or our breathing, we can move the energy within our spine up and down countless times as a spiritual exercise and thereby imitate the movements of the angels going in and out of Heaven. If you practice moving energy up and down your spine as in Jacob's ladder, which is a true stairway to Heaven, doing so will help with your spiritual practice.

A higher form of Jacob's ladder is as follows. While inhaling you should take the energy of your breath from your perineum through your tailbone and up your spine to the very top of your head. Exhaling as your abdomen contracts, you should then take that energy from the top of your head down the center of the front of your body through your abdomen to your perineum (located at the very bottom of your torso). Breathing in again you should send that energy up your spine into your head, and breathing out you guide it down the front of your body again to your perineum. Over and over again you must practice this throughout the day. You are basically guiding your energy in a loop around your body.

This is a simple method of leading your breathing in a circular orbit, and is a spiritual exercise that can be practiced during the idle moments of the day, or during a time of prayer. It is a spiritual practice just by itself. You can practice this throughout the day hundreds of times and it will gradually make your mind more clear. Then, like angels able to decipher the messages of Heaven, you will become better at intuiting the quietest inspirations of God. Elijah was able to do so only after his mind became quiet and he could then hear God's still, small voice of gentle whispering in the desert.

INTERNAL CONSECRATION

Across the world, religions regularly express a devout attitude before the divine, and as Christians we do so by making the sign of the cross where we touch our hand to the forehead, then to the chest and then to each shoulder. From earliest times Christians have made the sign of the cross, and Saint Basil the Great tells us that the apostles themselves taught it.

Making the sign of the cross on our body is an act of consecration in Christianity. By making the sign of the cross we acknowledge God's presence, protection and favor. It prepares us for receiving God's blessing and disposes us to acquire his grace. Making the sign of the cross is done externally, but if we trace out the outlines of the cross within our bodies then we will profess the central belief of our faith in a more interior fashion. Doing so will deeply identify us with the sacredness of the crucifixion and demonstrate our commitment to the truth of Christianity.

Therefore, this is another daily internal exercise we can practice that is part of the stage of purification and which will prepare us for receiving God's blessing of *theoria* and *theosis*. It involves using our internal energy to make the sign of the cross within our bodies over and over again, thereby sanctifying ourselves. Because this practice involves using our will to move our internal energy, it should remind us that we need to willingly sacrifice ourselves for our brethren through compassionate deeds of kindness just as it was Christ's will to sacrifice himself for us all by dying on the cross.

You should practice this energetic method of internal

consecration for fifteen minutes or longer, once or twice per day. The method is as follows.

Upon inhalation of a breath you lead the energy from the center of your palms and fingers to the center of your chest, remembering the Sacred Heart of Jesus. Upon an exhalation of your breathing you lead the energy from your chest center out across your arms and into the palms and fingers of both hands where Jesus was nailed to the cross. The pattern in your body is like the transept of a church.

Simultaneous to making these horizontal arms of the cross, upon an inhalation you imagine drawing into the top of your head the energies of the Holy Spirit in the form of a blessing. You imagine that this energy from the head descends into the center of your chest and then down into lower abdomen. During an exhalation you must push this energy from your lower abdomen through your legs to the bottom of each foot where Jesus was nailed to the cross. This creates the vertical *corpus* part of the cross within you.

These horizontal and vertical breathing circuits make a cross within the body that commemorates Christ's crucifixion. You can practice each of these breathing circuits separately, but must eventually join them together so that these two circuits are performed simultaneously in conjunction with your breathing.

While performing this internal consecration you have the option of also reciting "Amen." The "Ah-" syllable is mentally or quietly recited during your inhalations and the "-men" syllable is recited during exhalations when you push the energy to your feet and return it to your palms.

By daily performing this spiritual exercise you reaffirm the commitment within yourself to the process of *catharsis*. You also consecrate yourself by showing a willingness to receive Christ's blessings into your life. This exercise can be performed immediately after the practice of Jacob's ladder, or at a separate time, and should become a life-long practice to wash your inner spiritual body.

HEAVENLY RECOGNITION

Those who devote themselves to such practices are often rewarded with heavenly recognition for their efforts to remember Christ and his suffering.

Some will see the Sacred Heart of Jesus inside them as if in a vision. Others may sometimes feel a cool vapor enveloping their bodies that hovers around them like a light wind. It might also sometimes feel as if your feet were being washed with cool water just as Christ washed the feet of His disciples. Some may feel an anointing in the head like a baptism or blessing, or feel the blessings of the Holy Spirit moving in various parts of their body. Those who have struggled with celibacy, as a recognition of their efforts to remain chaste, will sometimes be rewarded by feelings as if their pelvis and groin were being washed by the Holy Spirit. Sometimes their hands, where Christ was nailed to the cross, can turn very hot or cold during *purgatio*, which may also happen to other parts of the body as well.

For those who grow in holiness and grace from their daily commitment to contemplation and such spiritual exercises, God will often bless them with other gentle reminders of the Holy Spirit as well.

CHAPTER 9

THE DAILY ABLUTION OF FOUR INTERNAL WASHINGS

In the Old Testament, an ablution was the prerequisite act of praying or washing oneself before approaching God in some way, such as prior to performing a sacrifice or entering a temple. The individual who aspires to *theoria* and then the *theosis* of union with God should similarly perform a special ablution every day in order to diminish the obstacles preventing greater communion with the Lord. This is the shortest way to spiritual sanctification.

Sanctification is both an act and a *process,* namely the collection of all your activities that prepare for the cleansing energies of the Holy Spirit to appear within yourself. These energies that will appear within your mind and body during the process of sanctification are the power behind the charisma of the saints, and are a necessary component of the pathway to *theosis.*

Some animals such as birds bathe themselves by

washing their bodies with dust, which means that they cleanse themselves with the earth element. Some animals wash themselves by using the wind element, allowing it to blow away the dirt that has collected on their bodies. Human beings wash themselves using the water element, but this external cleansing is not enough to purify the internal state of our bodies and minds. On the spiritual path we particularly need something that will internally wash both our minds and our vital energy, which is the breath of life given to us by our Maker. The pathway of glorification, deification or divinization that proceeds to *theosis* requires that we purify their nature through our spiritual practices.

By continually sacrificing worldly desires - such as we do through the practices of prayer, chanting, worship, mindfulness and meditation - by this means we become more pure in the eyes of God, and through these emptying and purifying practices we become ready to be filled with His grace. When we wash away our self-centered concerns by a longing for God along with a greater kindness and selfless service shown to others, we also achieve an internal purity of the heart and mind that can lead to *theoria*. By directing our will power to also wash the living energy of our bodies and souls, in this way we can directly prepare for the active rigors of *catharsis*, *theoria* and *theosis*.

On the spiritual path we must go beyond ordinary religious ceremonies to engage in innumerable intensified practices that prepare for the arrival of the Holy Spirit. Just as you can experience Apostle Paul's unceasing prayer after much prayer recitation, you can also experience an automatic internal washing within yourself by the energies of the Holy Spirit if you prepare for it. These blessed energies are involved in all three stages of divinization that we normally call spiritualization, sanctification, deification, glorification or *theosis*, especially during the stage of *catharsis* or *purgatio*, and we can invite this sanctifying grace into ourselves through proper Christian practice.

What is it like to experience these energies of *catharsis*?

Sister Maria Faustina Kowalska once wrote of her own experience, saying, "I was all afire, but without burning up ... I felt some kind of fire in my heart ... I was so enveloped in the great interior fire of God's love ... I feel I am all aflame. ... Today, a living flame of divine love entered my soul." She associated this purifying heat with her practice of mental silence, which is how one cultivates the holy stage of spiritual warming that precedes *theosis*.

The Christian nun, Abbess Hildegard of Bingen, reported: "When I was forty-two years and seven months old, Heaven was opened and a fiery light of exceeding brilliance came and permeated my whole brain, and inflamed my whole heart and whole breast, not like a burning but like a warming flame, as the sun warms everything with its rays touch. And immediately I knew the meaning of the exposition of the Scriptures ... though I did not have the interpretation of the words or their texts or the division of syllables or the knowledge of cases or tenses." (*Mystics of the Christian Tradition*, Steven Fanning, p. 83)

Saint Philip Neri often felt heat throughout his entire body during the stage of purgation. "It sometimes extended over his whole body, and for all his age, thinness and spare diet, in the coldest days of winter it was necessary, even in the midst of the night, to open the windows, to cool the bed, to fan him while in bed, and in various ways to moderate the great heat. Sometimes it burned his throat, and in all his medicines something cooling was generally mixed to relieve him. Cardinal Crescenzi said that sometimes when he touched his hand, it burned as if the saint was suffering from a raging fever. … Even in winter he almost always had his clothes open from the girdle upwards, and sometimes when they told him to fasten them lest he should do himself some injury, he used to say he really could not because of the excessive heat he felt. One day, at Rome, when a great quantity of snow had fallen, he was walking in the streets with his cassock unbuttoned; and when some of his penitents who were with him were hardly able to endure the cold, he laughed at them and said it was a shame for young men to feel cold when old men did not." (*God and the Evolving Universe*, Redfield, Murphy & Timbers, pp. 111-112).

Richard Rolle reported, "It was real warmth, too, and it felt as if it were actually on fire. I was astonished at the way the heat surged up, and how this new sensation brought great and unexpected comfort. I had to keep feeling my breast to make sure there was no physical reason for it! But once I realized that it came entirely from within, that this fire of love had no cause, material or sinful, but was the gift of my Maker, I was absolutely delighted, and wanted my love to be even greater. … If we put our finger near a fire we feel the heat; in much the same way a soul on fire with love feels, I say, a genuine warmth." (*The Fire of Love*, Clifton Wolters, pp. 88-89)

Just as Moses encountered the burning bush on Mount Sinai, during genuine *catharsis* you will experience an internal fire that will make your body hot all over, and your temperature will even rise. Your entire body will become like the bush on Mount Sinai that burned without actually burning. You will experience a similar heat within your body for days, and afterwards you will attain a sense of wonderful sweetness and quiet, or even hear heavenly music inside you.

A related experience is to often feel a warm current of energy flowing throughout your body that initiates you into some of the other processes of *catharsis* or purgation. This will be a real physical warmth that often produces a great feeling of comfort, although it will sometimes be uncomfortable due to the cleansing work it is performing. This is a warmth of love supplied by the Holy Spirit, a fire that internally purifies you and helps you to separate yourself from your mental defilements and passions. It is the *incendium amoris* of the Christian path brought about by your spiritual efforts at silence, mindfulness, prayer, chanting, obedience, and worship.

Everyone will experience *incendium amoris* differently, so have no fear if this spiritual warmth manifests in a different form than already described. Many variations are possible. *All the saints have experienced this inner heat blaze*, but only a few spoke of it openly such as Symeon the New Theologian, Theophan the Recluse, Saint Augustine, Bernard of Clairvaux, Hildegard of Bingen, John Tauler, Angela of Foligno, Catherine of Genoa, Macarius, Francisco de Osuna, Margery Kempe, Marie of the Incarnation, Madame Guyon, George Fox, and William Law. Each and every ecclesiastic who cultivates for true spiritual union with God *must go through this purgation* to reach the sweetness of the Holy Spirit. It is part of the entire process that leads to *theosis*.

These inner energy and heat phenomena are what one

can expect from the practices that prepare you for *theosis*, so have no fear. The warmth and heat you will experience are the natural initiatory process of true *catharsis* brought to you by the Holy Spirit in response to the intensity of your spiritual efforts. After you go through this purgation you will start to attain gnosis, the spiritual knowledge of a saint, which is knowledge of the divine. Gnosis brings insight into the spiritual and human realms, including insight into the affairs and minds of men. It is a transcendental and material understanding, a maturing of the powers of knowing produced from your rigorous efforts at prayer, mindfulness, meditation and contemplation.

Richard Rolle wrote, "I have found that to love Christ above all else will involve three things: warmth and song and sweetness. And these three, as I know from personal experience, cannot exist for long without there being great quiet." Therefore, it is essential for the attainment of *theosis* that you include meditation and quieting prayer in your daily activities as a preparation. Furthermore, *all your spiritual practices* must be looked at as a means of developing this required inner tranquility and calmness. It is only through internal serenity or stillness that one can achieve *theoria* and then progress to *theosis* and deification.

Our human knowledge is based on reflection, and because our gnosis of mental knowing is limited it can become a barrier between God and ourselves. Clinging to our thoughts is like idolatry in that it prevents us from experiencing *theoria* because we take our own concerns as of greater importance than God's presence. The remedy is a daily practice of the great quiet of meditation that washes away the noises of the intellect you normally hear in your head, which is something you will often experience after chanting or prayer as well.

Through this inner mental silence you can start to achieve a closer union with God, whose nature is peacefulness. However, we are to seek an internal mental purity that will not just bring us the spiritual union of *theoria*, but which will ignite the necessary spiritual fire of *purgatio* within us that will cleanse our bodies, thoughts, desires and attachments to make this possible.

God created Heaven and Earth, and is the light of Heaven and Earth. John told us directly that "God is light," and He guides His light to whomever He wills. *Theoria* is to abide in this light during spiritual practice until it brings about a more perfect union with God through the next spiritual stage of *theosis*.

One must work at their spiritual practices to touch this light, and must daily remain in this light until it produces the actual fire of purgation. Your spirit is of God and light, but the soul is divided into two parts. One part touches Heaven and the other is attached to the prison of the flesh. You must cleanse the part of the soul that clings to the human body through spiritual practices that sever your connection with the world. Through the purgation of *incendium amoris* you will then become cleansed and readied for God. Through the fire of purgation you will eventually become a being of light who inhabits a body while transcending the world.

The process of sanctification comes to a man or woman when, after much prior spiritual effort, heavenly grace descends upon them and starts washing them internally with the energies of Holy Spirit. How can you prepare for this necessity since this is the required pathway to *theosis*?

First, you must join the community in all its regular practices of prayer, silence, worship, chanting, meditation, contemplation, obedience and so forth.

Second, just as you would prepare for a guest by cleaning a room before their arrival, you can invite the arrival of the Holy Spirit by showing a willingness to purify yourself internally, just as you do by policing your inner thoughts in order to perfect your mind and behavior. In this case, to beckon the grace of the Holy Spirit that leads to *theosis* you can every day take a few moments to internally wash yourself with the very breath of life that God gave you, which is of the same nature as your soul. You can also mentally wash yourself with the pure celestial energies of the Heavens that God created to give us the light of illumination. One type of washing is for your body and soul, and another is for your spirit.

This daily bathing is done in four parts, and makes one more presentable to the Maker because it is a way of detaching yourself from worldly impurities and material attachments. The effort proves that you are willing to invite in the purifying grace of transformation required for divinization. God's grace is freely available to all, but He often waits to see if the person is willing to make the effort to please Him. Although we call it a daily washing, bathing, ablution or baptism, these exercises are as if you were placing yourself in a sacrificial altar where your worldly self and worldly desires will be burned away by the *purgatio* of the Holy Spirit.

THE FOUR STEPS

To receive such a blessing, you must every day wash

yourself with the elemental energies of God. Afterwards you must imagine being washed by light, namely the two celestial energies of the sun and moon that provide the Heavens with illumination. In both cases, you will wash yourself with what can be considered positive and negative or hot and cold energies, namely the fire and water element as well as sunlight and moonlight.

Just as you would get down on your knees and wash every nook and cranny of a monastery's floor to scrub it clean, you must daily move your internal energy everywhere within your physical body to wash yourself with that vital energy. By showing a willingness to perform this inner cleansing with the breath of life that God gave you, you will open a doorway for the grace of the Holy Spirit to more fully manifest within you. If you perform this additional work as an adjunct to your other spiritual practices, the work completed by this cleansing process will invite in the energies of the Holy Spirit that will spontaneously, like the Unceasing Prayer mentioned by the Apostle Paul, start strongly flowing inside you as an independent force of spiritual transformation.

To arouse your own internal energies for this ablution, an aspirant must first imagine that they wash themselves with water and fire, and should imagine actually *feeling* the energy movements purifying their body. Imagination or not, you must really try to make your internal energy feel a special way and step into those feelings just as athletes mentally rehearse their emotions and performance before competitions.

Just as elite athletes routinely use visualization practice as part of their training, where they mentally rehearse a performance by arousing the very same feelings and emotions they would normally experience during an athletic competition, you must try to feel the energies of fire and water actually moving around inside you and washing your body to purify it, thereby severing your attachments to the passions and sensual indulgences. In other words, you have to use your will to connect with your vital energy and move it in ways that simulate fire and water cleansing your body internally.

Afterwards, you must ask for divine grace in helping you wash your internal body again. This time you will use God's celestial energies that illuminate the Heavens, namely the light of the moon and sun. These energies are more refined and thus more akin to the energies of the spirit. The objective of this daily practice of ablution using heavenly and earthly forces is to help you truly purify your body, soul and spirit.

For this set of four ablutions, every part of your body must be mentally washed with the energy of hot fire and then cool water. You must imagine these energies flowing within you from bottom to top, and from top to bottom, cleansing you to produce a more purified state that is a precursor to *Homo Deus*. Psalm 66:12 tells us, "We went through fire and water, but you brought us to a refreshing place." Thus you will wash your body with these two energies in preparation for deification.

Afterwards you must imagine being bathed with the cooling lightness of soft moonlight spreading inside you, and then the bright warming energy of sunlight. You need to imagine that these energies wash your entire body like a baptism and transform it into infinite, transparent light that is one with the Creator and the universe. Hence, you must imagine flooding all parts of your body with these lights, feeling that all parts of your body become a unified whole of first moon energy and then sun energy, and then at the end of this visualization you should imagine becoming pure sunlight that shines everywhere infinitely. At that time you totally become just spirit by mentally give up the notion of possessing a body. Bodiless and incorporeal, you imagine that you are just light shining everywhere.

Here are more detailed instructions for this daily practice of four ablutions.

Sitting alone during a quiet time, you gradually imagine that your entire body becomes burning with a "happy fire." You first imagine that your feet start stirring with warm energy. Starting from the bottom of your right foot and proceeding upwards to your right leg, then left foot and left leg, right thigh and then left thigh, pelvis and trunk, arms and then head … You basically imagine that you progressively become a pillar of fire, for as Hebrews 12:29 says, "God is a consuming fire." You imagine that your body of fire, like the burning bush seen by Moses, is burning away all the impurities and defilements within you. You should also move the warm energy around within all your body parts to dissolve away any internal obstructions or blockages you feel stuck inside you. You must practice being gladsome and happy while doing this because this is a great purgation and purification act you are doing.

Therefore when you do this inside you, as you move the energy you should be joyful that you are burning away all the corruption within the flesh of your body and thereby freeing your soul from bodily attachments and corruption. While becoming purified by the flames, where you imagine that your body burns away, you must hold onto a feeling of great cheerfulness that the connection between your corrupt flesh and your soul is being purified. You should with gladness sacrifice that burning corruption as an offering to God.

While undergoing this burning, you should imagine that your bones within you turn a blazing whiteness because of the fire, and your outer body of flesh burns away until just the white bones of your skeleton are left sitting there, just like the bleached bones within an ossuary. Imagine that the fire consumes you until all that is left in place of your body is the white skeleton inside you just sitting there.

When doing this visualization exercise, you can imagine seeing all the bones within your body as bright white in color while your flesh surges with a hot energy just as happened to Richard Rolle, Philip Neri, Padre Pio and many other saints. This spiritual practice will help to initiate this necessary spiritual process of cleansing and transformation. After you imagine becoming an entire white skeleton, you must imagine that your skeleton turns into dust that then blows away so that you are incorporeal like empty space. Then you remain in that state of formless incorporeality to experience the peace of God.

This mental rehearsal prepares you for the arrival of the true spiritual fire of *purgatio* or *catharsis* that is the genuine purification produced by the Holy Spirit. It will be similar to the rehearsal you are imagining. In that stage of purification, which happens many years prior to the finality of glorification, you become like a burning bush that burns without burning. In your daily practice you must therefore imagine feeling a warmth and then heat (if possible) that burns away all of your muscles and flesh until all that is left are your white bones, and then just ashes that blow away.

Fire is the great purifier. *The Sayings of the Desert Fathers* accordingly records the following story. "Abba Lot came to Abba Joseph and said: Father, according as I am able, I keep my little rule, and my little fast, my prayer, meditation and contemplative silence; and, according as I am able, I strive to cleanse my heart of thoughts: now what more should I do? The elder rose up in reply and stretched out his hands to heaven, and his fingers became like ten lamps of fire. He said: Why not become fire?"

Ashes to ashes, dust to dust, after the indwelling spirit is liberated then our bodies return to dust. After you imagine that your body turns into dust during this spiritual practice you then imagine that you retain your awareness but become formless pristine empty space.

Each individual will perform this visualization a bit differently with the commonality that you must eventually imagine that all your bones, organs, muscles, tendons and flesh eventually burn with a joyful and playful energy, a thrilling elated energy, a delightful cheerful energy, or glorious exhilarating energy that you feel inside you energizing everything.

In other words, you must try to stimulate joy and warm energetic feelings inside you during this purification practice. All your body parts are to be enervated by the warmth and heat of fire as well as joy, and you must imagine that your bones eventually shine with a brilliant light and energy. After everything is burned away you imagine becoming empty space and then must rest in that mental state of peace just as you do when your mind calms from prayers or chanting.

After you are done resting as empty space and feel an internal urge to start again, you imagine that your body returns to normal, and that you are once again a body rather than formless empty space. Now you start to imagine that a stream of cool water enters the top of your head and descends within you, permeating all your tissues and purifying them. Imagine feeling it coating everything inside your body even to the bottom of your feet. Starting from the crown of your head you imagine that you are being washed with a water of purification that touches everything within you to help wash away any remaining impurities that the fire of purgation left behind. Imagine that it is a gift of heavenly assistance, an internal baptism to help purify you through yet another cathartic washing.

From the top of your head you must imagine feeling that cooling spring water starts pouring into you and flows everywhere inside you to wash all the sections of your body, restoring you to the perfection you once had as a younger pure spirit. These purifying waters are like a baptismal blessing from above, like a grace received from Heaven. Using your mind, lead the energy of the waters everywhere inside you to cleanse all your body parts so that you become internally resplendent and pure. All uncleanliness within you is to be washed with a watery coolness so that a spiritual body within becomes pure like transparent crystal.

Individuals who practice this may often feel during regular hours that their body becomes enveloped in a cool vapor that surrounds them, and which seems to rise into the air. This heavenly coolness is a gift from the Holy Spirit, and it also occurs to aspirants who engage in other spiritual practices too. Here, as with the fire of purgation, we are simply imitating the effects that Heaven will bring to us in order to hasten their arrival and move more quickly through *catharsis* to *theoria* and then *theosis.*

This water should be imagined as pouring into you from the top of your head, and you must lead it to penetrate everywhere, even into your arms, hands, legs, feet and genitalia – basically all the different sections and parts of your body. Use your mind to wash your entire body with cool water, and *feel* that movement of energy within yourself. However, instead of joy you must hold onto an attitude of humility and gratefulness during this internal water baptism. After reaching your feet, you should imagine that any dirt or filth exudes out from your toes and the bottom of your soles to leave your body forever. Then you should pause in refrain.

Numbers 31:23 instructs us, "anything that can stand the fire must be put through the fire and then it shall become clean. Nevertheless it must also be purified with the water of purification." This helps to explain these two practices. After completing this spiritual exercise and resting a practitioner starts again, but differently.

After washing your body inside with the earthly energies of fire and water, it is time to wash yourself with higher celestial energies that are more purified and refined. It is time to wash yourself with the higher heavenly octaves of fire and water energy since those are more appropriate to your own spiritual nature. Therefore in this next phase you imagine that the light of our two foremost celestial bodies penetrates your body to effect a second but higher washing of your body and spirit. First, you must imagine that you become filled with the light of the moon that cleanses you, and lastly you envision that you become a light like that of the sun.

Our soul partakes of both male and female natures that

are the Divine within us. However, the pure male and female energies become corrupted when encased within the human garment of flesh. The light of the sun and moon are akin to pure forms of our masculine and feminine natures, which is why these celestial energies are used in the daily ablution of internal washing. Our masculine and feminine natures within us must be washed over and over again before they can reach a harmonious state of purity and union that matches the uncorrupted and undivided wholeness of the divine.

As Saint Francis of Assisi intimated for us in *Canticle of Brother Sun and Sister Moon*, these energies can bring about a transformation of our inner natures just as they bring about transformations in Nature itself. Therefore, first we will wash ourselves with moonlight, and remain passively waiting bathed in internal moonlight until it slowly transforms and becomes resplendent sunlight.

How do we actually do this?

Just as Jesus washed the feet of his disciples with cool water, first imagine that the pure soft light of the moon starts to enter into you through your left foot and by degrees (left foot, right foot, left leg, right leg, ...) passes upwards throughout your body until your entire body is filled with cool white moonlight, purifying and shining through all your bones and flesh. You must imagine that even your bones shine with a beautiful white lunar light, soft and gentle, that envelops your entire body.

Slowly this moonlight should change into blazing sunlight that becomes a piercing light streaming from your every pore. So bright is this sunlight that you become a brilliant splendor yourself, shining forth in rays of light that penetrate everywhere unopposed. You must imagine that the brilliance of this light is so great that you become bodiless light again, which is the body's spiritual essence. After being bathed in moonlight you become just light.

1 John 1:5 says "God is light," so you are now imagining that you become the essence of all things, which is light. Visualize that you become an immeasurable body of light, and by this practice allow the illusion of being a solid body to completely disappear so that you are just bodiless light. Allow your sense of identity to become free of all constraints so that it is no longer confined to being a body of flesh.

At this point, you should let go of the consciousness of being in a body and rest in being only boundless light - transparent, pure, incorporeal, infinite, everywhere. The soul is a prisoner of the material world and material concerns, and in this step of imagining that you become only light you must free it from clinging to any remaining material restraints or desires, just as you strive to do during regular monastic life. You must forget your body and imagine that you become pure immaterial light, where nothing is manifest, and thus you become incorporeal and perfect even as your Father in Heaven is perfect.

So, you first filled yourself with moonlight to wash yourself with feminine energies, stayed in that light and slowly let the moonlight turn into sunlight, masculine in nature, and now you must give up the sense of being a body so that you are only light. Previous to this you did as Luke 3:16 stated, "I indeed baptize you with water, but one mightier than I ... shall baptize you with the Holy Spirit and with fire."

It is through a daily practice of these Four Ablutions that purify you with fire and water, and then baptize you with moonlight and sunlight, that you will slowly purify yourself. In this way you will prepare yourself for the transformations required of purgation, *theoria* and *theosis*. In time those transformations will automatically occur within you such as spontaneous manifestations of internal heat, currents of energy running within you, and other purifying blessings from the Holy Spirit as reported to us by our Church Fathers, elders and saints.

Repeated purification by daily ablution *is* the road of transcendence. These Four Washings will surely lead to the arrival of the Holy Spirit and then the Fountain of Life of glorification. They can be the difference between those who achieve *theosis* or not. Once again, here is a summary of the four steps of this practice.

PRACTICE EVERY DAY

The ultimate purpose of humankind is eventual union with God, which we call divinization, glorification, deification or *theosis*. God wants all of us to achieve *theosis*, but few wish to consistently make the efforts that lead to *theosis*. Our preoccupation with the world and desire for material things stands in the way. Yet often the effort is not undertaken simply because people lack guidance on how to proceed.

Theosis is the ultimate purpose of the monastic life, so many answer His calling to enter the Holy life with this objective in mind. However, they fail in their efforts because they don't know what they should practice and how they should practice or conduct themselves.

God wants us to achieve *theosis* in this very life rather than wait for deification in the hereafter. The daily four washings quickens our sanctification by purifying us for the visitation of the Holy Spirit because you rehearse the actual processes you will pass through during *catharsis* and then will start experiencing them due to your pre-work. By simulating the processes of purgation you will actually be stimulating and performing the processes of purgation. You will thus beckon the Holy Spirit to help you through this preparatory work.

The human soul suffers discontent not just because of the pains of living, but because over time it becomes more and more divorced from its spiritual self and longs to return to its original purity. This is why many people devote themselves to God through prayer and the monastic tradition. The soul can only reach felicity again when it purges itself of its lower nature to reveal the full potential of a transcendental promise - an existence of total purity and bliss that is your fundamental birthright from God. However, the soul can only achieve this by detaching itself from its imperfect physical container and its preoccupation with worldly matters.

Clement of Alexandria in his work *Paedagogus* wrote, "Being baptized, we are illuminated; illuminated we become children [lit. 'sons']; being made children, we are made perfect; being made perfect, we become immortal."

We can and should therefore practice on a daily basis this method of internal baptism, a series of ablutions that will help us achieve *theosis* by placing us directly within the process of *catharsis*. Man must guide his own inward light and direct it towards the efforts of purification and restoration. In response to our own willingness to stop identifying with our body and our efforts to mentally free ourselves from material concerns, the light of God will begin to shine more brightly within us and eventually invite the Holy Spirit to complete the task of ascension.

For this method of internal baptism you imagine that your body becomes engulfed with fire, proceeding from your feet upwards, while entering into a happy state of mind. You then mentally wash yourself with the energy of fresh water descending downwards from your head to the bottom of your feet while entering into a mental state of cleanliness, thankfulness and humility. Here you go through fire and water to arrive at a refreshing condition.

You then fill yourself with soft moonlight until every cell and pore of your body, especially your bones, shines with soft white moonlight. Mentally the moonlight should slowly transform into sunlight, and you finally imagine becoming that sunlight and only that light, without a material nature, and then you should mentally rest in that state of formless non-corporeality.

This is one of the exercise sets that speedily brings about *catharsis* when performed every day. It works because you are emulating the fires of purgation, and that exertion invites the holy presence into you because you are showing a willingness for purgation and doing the actual work of purification. Your other practices of prayer, mindfulness, chanting, obedience, meditation and so forth prepare you for *catharsis*, but many individuals do not achieve it for lack of taking these additional steps to purify themselves as the Bible has indicated.

Baptism is "the gateway to life in the Spirit" and we practice for this spiritual baptism through all our spiritual practices. That includes these mental washings to cleanse our impurities through the power of His energies and light.

True baptism in the Holy Spirit is to be blessed by the

spiritual energies of transformation, and this is a second step after the Sacrament of Holy Baptism with water and oil that lays the foundation of the Christian life. Christ said to Nicodemus, "I can guarantee this truth. No one can enter the kingdom of God without being born of water and the Spirit." Here we emulate this process in order to receive the gift of the Holy Spirit.

The Apostle Paul writes, "Know you not that your bodies are the temples of God and that the Spirit of God dwells within you?" (1 Cor. 3:16). We are not bodies but souls, and the soul is of the same essence as God. The soul, however, is entombed in layers of coverings, namely the body, mind, and the intellect. It is the indwelling soul that is alive rather than its coverings, which our soul clings to out of habit, but one can use the powers or energies of the soul to purify its coverings so that it can ultimately detach from those attachments and transcend the world as *Homo Deus*.

Over time our souls collect pollution because we become so identified with these coverings of body and mind that we no longer have any idea that we are souls. But, once we begin washing our body and mind in this way it will move us toward the inherent purity of our souls, and we will begin to free ourselves from attachments to these coverings. We will start freeing our soul from being bound by earthly corruption. As Psalm 66:12 told us, after going through fire and water we will reach a refreshing place.

In particular, when you wash yourself with fire you should adopt a mood of happiness while imagining that your body entirely burns away all the impurities inside it. Mentally washing yourself with water should be accompanied by an attitude of gratefulness and humility.

At the subsequent stage of washing through light you should first imagine that you are filled with feminine lunar energy, and then solar light energy. Then you become just light itself where you are bodiless without a torso. You are then just formless light generously offering yourself to the entire universe. You must imagine that you become infinite immaterial sunlight that universally shines everywhere with transparent clarity.

These four ablutions will help you sever your connections with gross materiality and attain a more heavenly state. Those who practice these purifications in order to attain *theosis* will become endowed with a luminous splendor due to their efforts, and because of those efforts the divine light will further bestow upon them additional heavenly aid for the attainment of *theoria* and *theosis*. It is because you make the effort that extra help will arrive.

Man's consciousness is the very highest within this world, but a qualitative change is required to ascend yet higher. The soul can only go higher if it drops its attachments to the physical world by transcending its carnal, animalistic and materialistic tendencies. The souls of the gnostics, elders and saints, after leaving their bodies, ascend even above the angelic realm to enjoy proximity to the Supreme Light because they have worked to purify themselves of all their faults and attachments. Perfect consciousness is full of light and bliss, and we enter the monastic life in order to proceed through a structured process of purgation that quickly leads to *theoria* and then the *theosis* of spiritual union characterized by bliss and light.

You must therefore do this practice every day, and like watering one's garden the results will grow.

CHAPTER 10

LECTIO DIVINA

Saint Padre Pio once said, "Through the study of books one seeks God; by meditation one finds him."

This type of spiritual meditation he recommends is "devoid of content" or "empty of thoughts" while another form of meditation, known as contemplation, is absolutely preoccupied by thoughts and conceptions. However, some groups use the words differently and define "meditation" as mental consideration (the pondering of a meaning that requires the use of your intellect) while "contemplation" is taken as a quiet thoughtlessness and humility in the presence of God that is often referred to as emptiness meditation.

There are also forms of spiritual prayer and spiritual communion that are empty of thought, such as centering prayer that is basically a practice of inner silence, whereas ordinary prayer is filled with the narrative self-talk of our intellect. The *Lectio Divina* method of studying the Bible to understand its message specifies how to conduct oneself with this type of thoughtful prayer that can become a conversation with God to help guide our life, and which is then followed by a quiet time without inner self-talk.

How should we therefore study Scripture and then pray? Through *Lectio Divina,* which is a formula for transforming our understanding, and ultimately ourselves, according to the indications of Scripture and then prayer. *Lectio Divina* involves both contemplation and meditation.

A Carthusian friar, Guigo II, wrote *The Ladder of Monks* introducing *Lectio Divina*, although it may have been used prior to his account. The method of *Lectio Divina* specifies four steps that produce a ladder of prayer based on reading Scripture: *lectio* (reading), *meditatio* (meditation), *contemplatio* (contemplation), and *oratio* (prayer). Therefore, *Lectio Divina* has four separate steps: read; meditate; contemplate; and pray.

First a passage of Scripture is read – there is a slow and quiet reading of God's Word. Then the meaning of the text is reflected upon through pondering so that you reach a preliminary level of understanding. Just as the Virgin Mary "pondered in her heart," you ruminate on the passage until you perceive a higher understanding of the text. You might also sit with a passage and slowly repeat it over and over again until its meaning is very clear.

Afterwards, this is not followed by more analysis or intellectual ponderings. Rather, this is followed by the peaceful approach of internally quieting yourself. Within that stillness you open yourself up to allow inspirations about the text to arise within you from the Holy Spirit that might reveal a higher meaning.

In other words, after reading a spiritual passage and

thinking about it you then put your thoughts away, you wait in humble silence expecting nothing (which is one of the keys to nourishing Christian spirituality), and then sometimes a revolutionary insight will arise within you due to divine inspiration. By resting in silence without exerting your ego and will, you will break your prejudiced ways of thinking, and that opening of silence can produce space enough for God's spirit to inspire you with new understanding. If two people are talking at the same time, on the other hand, they certainly won't be able to understand one another.

In John 14:27 Jesus said: "Peace I leave with you; my peace I give unto you." Therefore, during this third step of *contemplatio* you don't practice thinking, but practice a quiet communion with God after analyzing the passage. You put thinking aside and open yourself up to a full acceptance of the text by quieting your mind and resting in the presence of God, letting God fill you with His Spirit. Sometimes He will provide a spontaneous inspiration on some aspect of the passage, an understanding that may seem to bubble up out of nowhere, and sometimes you will just enjoy the peaceful silence until you are inspired to move on. You don't have to do anything but just allow the Spirit to act while you rest in tranquility. We don't want to think about the text at this stage otherwise we will be dominating the conversation.

As explained, sometimes during that short period of quiescence you will just experience the peace of His Spirit rather than any specific inspiration. At other times you might experience a spontaneous series of thoughts or determination that will be related to the passage. Thus, this is a quiet stage of spiritual communion where you empty yourself of your thoughts, and yet remarkable thoughts may sometimes spontaneously arise during this silence.

Lectio Divina is a process that moves you from an internal conversation or consideration into a communion with God where you assimilate the word of God. It is a movement into silence, and then back to expression again. You read a portion of text, decipher its meaning, engage in quiet reflection, and then go back and read more text as appropriate. Afterwards you end *Lectio Divina* with prayer.

Therefore, to consummate your understanding after a period of inner silence, through prayer you then speak to God, as you would with a friend, and request Him to help you incorporate into your life the message you have derived from reflective consideration. In Luke 10:37 Jesus said, "Go and do likewise," which means that after gaining an appropriate spiritual understanding about some passage, we should then incorporate the message into our life through our actions.

The purpose of *Lectio Divina* is therefore to apply spiritual understanding in your daily life, for that is the entire purpose of our spiritual literature – that we incorporate its message within our life and being. The root of the virtuous life is continuous study and application of the divine word. The study of Scripture obligates us to incorporate its teachings into our lives.

At the conclusion of study and reflection we are to pray to God to help us transform ourselves in line with the Holy message, or to request help in incorporating its principles into our life. Since every Biblical passage has different lessons, every prayer will be different. As with mindfulness practice where we recognize our errors from self-inspection, this recognition of what we need to do to better ourselves is how we can gradually purify ourselves for *theosis*.

When we are reading the New Testament, the passages often prompt us to imitate the example of Christ in our behavior, such as by imitating His virtues and doing good works. By undertaking such endeavors, we slowly exemplify Him and his efforts in the world. "Loving thy neighbor" is not supposed to be just idle talk, but the partaking of good deeds to help the world. We emulate Christ and become like Christ by demonstrating kindness, care, concern and compassion for others. It is through service to others that we can learn self-sacrifice as Christ demonstrated for us on the cross, and through those efforts we can make the world a better place as Christianity has intended.

In earlier times, monastery practice consisted of three elements: liturgical prayer, manual labor and *Lectio Divina*. The brethren had specified periods of manual labor as well as scheduled times for prayerful reading. *Lectio Divina* alongside the daily celebration of liturgy and prayer became a major pillar of spiritual practice, and the essential method of self-improvement for the goal of Christian perfection. This is the purpose of *Lectio Divina* for today – to accept instructions from the Bible on spiritual principles, and then to institute them in our lives.

Again, after a slow and thoughtful reading of Scripture, a practitioner then thinks about the reading, sometimes even visualizing the story within the passage or its message. You could read Scripture privately or listen to it in a group, you can focus on either a simple sentence or an entire passage that impresses you, but you must then follow the remaining steps of *Lectio Divina*. You must always ponder its meaning, and then subsequently engage in quiet meditation on the text that is "devoid of content." You must enter into a quiet mental stillness that, through the silencing of your ego, opens your mind enough to receive the presence of God or any message.

This is a state of tranquil repose where you put aside thoughts, an inner silence that often allows for a spontaneous spiritual inspiration to appear. It is a stage of quiet contemplation guided by the Holy Spirit, which may or may not inspire you with a message of higher spiritual understanding. In many cases the Spirit simply wishes you to rest in Peace rather than to give you thoughts, and this is also wholly appropriate.

Afterwards we must try to incorporate the message we derive into our daily life, which sometimes means that we should in some way imitate Christ's behavior. As you study the teachings of the Bible and apply them in your life it will transform you, and should move you towards the ideal of Christian perfection. Knowledge and understanding are barren unless they bear fruit in your character and behavior so here is the time when we try to derive spiritual instructions from the Bible so that we can apply them in our life.

Hence the goal of *Lectio Divina* is not simply intellectual understanding, but to find a deeper meaning within Scripture and then apply it within ourselves. Christian perfection entails the pursuit of a nobility of personality, values, thinking and behavior that you might call "consummate conduct" or a "conversion of manners." This irreproachable or elegant conduct is the desired perfection of Christianity, and this task of rectitude and purification requires prayer on our part.

Saint Clare of Assisi offered a different four-step sequence to prayer where you would first gaze on the cross (*intueri*), consider (*considerare*), contemplate (*contemplari*) and then imitate (*imitare*). The general pattern, applied to scriptural study, is that you might first read a passage from the Bible or visually remember one of its stories, ponder/consider its content and meaning, immediately afterwards engage in quiet thought-free meditation, and then try to incorporate the meaning you have derived or new inspiration that has developed into your daily life.

We study Scriptures to find guidance for a higher life, such as the proper patterns for our thoughts and behavior. By reading Scripture we slowly acquire wisdom, insight and understanding of how we should live for ourselves, and for the benefit of others in society. Then we practice prayer and mindfulness to keep on track.

However, wisdom is not limited to Scripture alone, and an aspirant can and should seek wisdom from other sources not normally considered spiritual works. One need not restrict themselves to the Bible or writings of the saints and Church Fathers to find practical wisdom for daily life.

The ultimate goal is to improve ourselves and become able to help others. We come to the monastic life to deny the world, but we also need to master the world for our needs and to service others through good works. However, how else is one to gather new knowledge, learn new skills, or simply understand the world and become able to transform it if they never pass beyond the gate of Scripture?

Monasteries have always been preserves of learning. Preserving (and learning) knowledge beyond the Scriptures has always been a mainstay of the monastic tradition.

Therefore, you should read widely beyond Scripture, and should not feel guilty for doing so. You need to expand your horizons in order to be able to better help people and transform the world. You should also strive to master skills other than those required of the religious vocation since they can be used to help others. If you are a cook for a monastery it is proper to keep learning better recipes and cooking methods for the benefit of your brothers, and if you must farm for the community's needs it is proper to seek advice from others more knowledgeable in this field. Where is one to find such knowledge in Scripture? You must seek elsewhere.

Do not restrict your study to Scripture alone but seek other sources than can help you develop more useful skills, teach you how to change your habits, teach you how to transform your personality to become a better person, teach you how to do things for the community's benefit and teach you how to develop better relationships with others.

If possible, read widely beyond the confines of religion to broaden your perspectives and avoid becoming stale through immersion in religious literature alone. Scripture is the pathway we have chosen to accomplish the task of self-perfection, self-improvement and *theosis* that produce *Homo Deus* and our return to the Father, but other sources are also available that teach the many worldly skills we need to survive and thrive, so use them. Be not ashamed or dissuaded from reading non-spiritual books, or desiring to master certain skills that might interest you. There is no sin in desiring to learn more skills and adding more variety to your spiritual life because this is the essence of self-improvement and self-perfection.

CHAPTER 11

THE NEED TO EXERCISE AND HOW TO REDUCE SEXUAL DESIRES

Most monasteries require that the monks and nuns work hard to support their institution, and this physical labor is also necessary to keep the balance right between work and prayer within monasteries and convents. It helps to pay the bills and keep everyone's body fit. However, as we age various health concerns will usually arise due to either poor diets or not enough exercise of the type that would stave off physical decline. Too many clerics, mendicants and monastics live sedentary lifestyles that cause them to fall short in these respects.

Therefore, over time all monks, nuns, priests and others engaged in the holy life should certainly be sure to eat nutritious foods, rather than harming themselves with extreme ascetic deprivation, and should engage in exercises that will improve their strength, flexibility, energy and core stability. For those on ascetic paths, they should take pains that the rigors of asceticism do not destroy their bodies, for they are temples of the spirit.

As mankind has progressed over the ages we have introduced new foods into our diets from far away places. We have discovered new medicines, technologies, labor saving devices, and even new forms of exercise that are highly beneficial for us. Why then should we not adopt foreign advances into our spiritual practices too, and thereby make our spiritual struggles easier even if those foreign innovations might initially seem quite alien?

The strangeness we feel upon first encountering new things is usually due to unfamiliarity and novelty. It is not due to the fact that they aren't good for us and won't benefit us. It is natural to try new things, such as new food dishes, and to readily adopt them into our lives when they are beneficial.

Therefore, whether they be foreign or domestic born, it is always proper and *even mandatory* that we adopt new practices into our established spiritual routines, or change our routines entirely, when we find something much better than what we are doing. This especially holds for our routines of spiritual practices since they are the core of our purpose. In any endeavor we want to become more sure of achieving the final objective, so it is natural that we might adopt new practices that will increase our chances at success. We should not reject innovative advances in our ways of doing things, which applies to our spiritual practices as well and our target of *theosis*, which is *Homo Deus*.

Through the ecclesiastical calling we have already chosen to make spiritual practice the central core aspect of our life in order to regain the real self that sleeps within us.

But are our spiritual efforts taking us anywhere? Are we making any spiritual progress in freeing ourselves from material captivity? If something improves our way of life within the Christian tradition by helping us better tread the pathway of *catharsis* to *theoria* and then *theosis*, then it is our duty to adopt it so that we might better handle our spiritual struggles, make more spiritual progress, and so that more people can actually achieve the objective of *theosis* and *Homo Deus*.

In particular, it is difficult to keep one's mind on God when personal heath issues arise, or when we must administer to the health needs of others in the community, so we must daily act to prevent such problems that would stand in the way of spiritual pursuits. If we can find practices that will reduce our community health issues, or help us handle our other spiritual trials and tribulations, then we should adopt them into our practice traditions even if they come from elsewhere or do not appear in the Rules of our orders. We must learn to respect our bodies by practicing the very best methods of self-maintenance that keep us fit and independent, otherwise we will become a burden for the rest of our community. For instance, if as a monk we don't maintain our physical fitness we will negatively influence a monastery as a whole.

Ecclesiastics all aspire to the holy life, but tend to live passive sedentary lives because of their immersion in prayer. Were they to commonly participate in daily flexibility exercises, they could reduce many difficulties caused by aging and the sedentary lifestyle, which will in turn eliminate many of the physical problems commonly seen in monasteries, convents and abbeys. We should always be seeking not just better health for our brethren but methods that will reduce the costs of health care and the service obligations that burden our communities. The problems are eminently preventable. Hence, everyone should try to participate in an exercise program to enhance their health and quality of life.

Because many monks, nuns and priests neglect regular exercise, ill health is often a direct or indirect result. The physical problems that are either directly or indirectly caused due to insufficient exercise usually develop slowly over a long period of time and go unnoticed, and then they can cascade into a crisis all at once. When the problems start to cause obvious physical symptoms it is often too late to cure ourselves, so *prevention is the proper strategy.*

Prevention requires a regular exercise program, but we should seek a certain kind that is most beneficial to our spiritual efforts. Regular stretching practice, for instance, will prevent the potentially disastrous results of insufficient exercise because it will strengthen the body and help us to maintain flexibility. It can also be used as an aid to the spiritual path, which is a fact discovered by the spiritual practitioners of the East.

In India the monks of various traditions have found a solution to health issues and the lack of exercise through the practice of gentle yoga that stretches the body, while in China the monks of various traditions have found a solution in the more active martial arts. These are alternatives to the typical ascetic means of driving the physical flesh to exhaustion in order to temper an unsubmissive body.

Taijiquan, baguaquan and *xingyiquan*, and Shaolin *kung-fu* exercises are the most beneficial exercises for spiritual practice discovered by the Chinese over the centuries. A famous Indian monk visited a group of Shaolin monks centuries ago, and then taught them the simple exercise routine of *Yi Jin Jing* in order to help them preserve their health since he observed they were weak and sickly due to a lack of physical exercise. He created this simple solution for a problem that certainly applies to our own monasteries and convents. Since that time, many simple-to-perform martial arts routines have been developed for monks and nuns to keep them in good shape.

Both yoga and the martial arts will not only help us maintain our health but are alternatives to prostrations in that they can often more effectively channel the passions of our younger members who are ridden with sexual desires they cannot yet control. Yoga and the martial arts can help Christian men direct those energies into exercises that will rechannel their inner vitality. With better health, and by using exercises to help pave the way, it will also become easier for the blessings of the Holy Spirit to appear and bring about *theoria* and *theosis*.

Therefore priests, monks and nuns should, on a daily basis, practice yoga and/or the martial arts. By yoga we mean hatha yoga, Pilates or Ginastica Natural (natural gymnastics that are a type of gymnastical yoga in motion). One should in particular practice the *kumbhaka* breath retention techniques of yoga that were designed to rechannel sexual desires through deep breathing that helps disperse it, and which produce a clarity of mind that will aid your spiritual practices. If your thoughts have already lead to sexual arousal, a monk or nun can use quick breathing (exhaling through the mouth more than inhaling) to relieve it. Yoga stretching practices can also help to handle many sexual difficulties that we face.

For instance, one remedy to practice before bedtime is the "flying bird" form of yoga and the martial arts that prevents wet dreams and nightly ejaculations that plague men. To practice the technique, stand straight like a tree. While inhaling, rise on your toes and bring the arms from your side to touch above your head. As you perform inhalation, pull the energy from your pelvis into your sacrum and upwards through your spine into your head. While rising on your feet, also look upwards at your hands that are being brought together to touch one another above your head. Upon exhalation, slowly come back down to rest on your feet again while simultaneously bringing your arms back down to your sides. Essentially, you pull the energy from your pelvis into your head through your spine while rising on your toes and raising your arms like wings, and then descend while exhaling and letting go. If wet dreams bother you then you should repeat this three to five times just before bedtime. The martial arts routines that priests, monks and nuns should practice basically link together in a series many simple movements like this.

The problem of sexual desire is sure to initially plague all celibates in the holy life, and the standard remedy is to avoid overeating and to reduce your food intake (such as through fasting), to fatigue the body (such as through hard work or prostrations), to keep away from any influences or lines of thought that might sprout into sexual desire, and to turn to prayer repetitions when lustful thoughts arise that won't go away. Some monasteries, such as those on Mount Athos in Greece, ban the entrance of woman so that sexual desires do not arise due to the presence of women. Needless to say, everyone should ban any access to internet pornography as well. Some spiritual traditions ban certain foods such as garlic, leeks and onions because they are said to give rise to sexual inclinations. Indians commonly use Asafoetida spice as an onion-garlic substitute.

Priests, monks and nuns shouldn't try to match any lustful inclinations or urges with their body when sexual desires arise, but should strive to remain pure like a newborn baby when carnal impulses assault them. If they can remain detached from sexual impulses when they arise and let them pass over them despite their assault then the urges will eventually pass away. However, if they eat overly nutritious foods when desires plague them, they're likely to stimulate their vitality and exacerbate the problem. While the standard remedy is restraint and less food (or even fasting) and praying until it passes, other traditions have found that a rechanneling of human energies into these special exercise routines is most helpful and productive in solving these issues and many other problems. Their adoption is warranted.

Hence, a program of martial arts, yoga and pranayama are recommended for all seminaries, monasteries and convents even though this may seem revolutionary for certain traditions. These are effective solutions that others have found, who were plagued with the same problems, but who lived so far away from us that their remedies never reached the founders of our traditions. But that does not mean we should not adopt them into our lives now that we have discovered they are powerful remedies. For cardio exercise, many monastics and clerics rightfully participate in the domestic sports of basketball and soccer.

Refrigeration replaced the ice block ... who cares who

invented it? Light bulbs and antibiotics were at one time revolutionary but now we all use them. The printing press at one time did not exist, nor did credit cards and cellphones. But now we have all adopted them due to their convenience even though they were invented elsewhere. There is not only an expected benefit to health when ecclesiastics start practicing yoga and the martial arts, but there will be some solutions to the issue of rechanneling sexual desires to deal with this troublesome issue.

Some monastics, mendicants and ascetics have recommended hitting your legs and hips with rattan bundles when sexual desires arise because this can distract your attention from such impulses. This is an excellent remedy for keeping their body chaste, but a higher solution is to rechannel your energies into physical activities that might also use up those impulses by tiring you out. Once you fall asleep, the problem is over for the day and may not appear on the morrow.

Chinese *taijiquan, baguaquan, xingyiquan*, (basically the "soft" martial arts that deal with controlling your inner energy that often turns into sexual desire when unmanaged), Shaolin *kung-fu* and Indian yoga stretches are a better long-term response with countless benefits to those living a spiritual life. They provide the solution to health maintenance issues as well. When practiced in a group, they also produce the same type of group camaraderie and community feeling as experienced during chanting. They should be adopted within all our monastic traditions.

It is hard for established monastery and convents to take on new traditions such as this, but it should be done. The martial arts and yoga should also be taught in our seminaries so that practitioners can take the techniques into our monasteries, abbeys and convents and help improve the health and welfare of Christian spiritual adherents.

Printed in Great Britain
by Amazon

16042883R00078